Say It
Right in
CHINESE

Second Edition

Easily Pronounced Language Systems

Clyde Peters, Author

New York Chicago San Francisco Lisb.. .. Madrid .. ..ty
Milan New Delhi San Juan Seoul Singapore Sydney

1 2 3 4 5 6 7 8 9 10 11 12 13 14 15   QFR/QFR   1 9 8 7 6 5 4 3 2 1

ISBN   978-0-07-176773-6
MHID   0-07-176773-8

Library of Congress Cataloging-in-Publication Data

Say it right in Chinese / Easily Pronounced Language Systems — 2nd ed.
       p.   cm. — (Say it right)
    Includes index.
    Text in English and Chinese and Chinese characters.
    ISBN 978-0-07-176773-6 (alk. paper)
    1. Chinese language—Pronunciation by foreign speakers.   2. Chinese language—Textbooks for foreign speakers—English.   3. Chinese language—Spoken Chinese.   I. Easily Pronounced Language Systems.   II. Clyde E. Peters, Author.

    PL1209.S28   2011
    495.1′83421—dc22   2011011057

Clyde Peters, author
Luc Nisset, illustrations
Betty Chapman, EPLS contributor, www.isayitright.com
Priscilla Leal Bailey, senior series editor
Lining Berman, Chinese consultant
Zhen Xie and **W. David Chen**, Chinese language consultants
Hong Chen, Chinese character consultant

Also available:
Say It Right in French, Second Edition
Say It Right in Italian, Second Edition
Say It Right in Spanish, Second Edition

For more titles and apps, see page 179.

Perfect your pronunciation by listening to sample phrases from this book. Go to www.audiostudyplayer.com, launch the Study Player, and then select: Chinese>For Travel>Say It Right in Chinese.

McGraw-Hill books are available at special quantity discounts to use as premiums and sales promotions or for use in corporate training programs. To contact a representative, please e-mail us at bulksales@mcgraw-hill.com.

This book is printed on acid-free paper.

CONTENTS

INTRODUCTION

The SAY IT RIGHT FOREIGN LANGUAGE PHRASE BOOK SERIES has been developed with the conviction that learning to speak a foreign language should be fun and easy!

All SAY IT RIGHT phrase books feature the EPLS Vowel Symbol System, a revolutionary phonetic system that stresses consistency, clarity, and above all, simplicity!

Since this unique phonetic system is used in all SAY IT RIGHT phrase books, you only have to learn the VOWEL SYMBOL SYSTEM ONCE!

The SAY IT RIGHT series uses the easiest phrases possible for English speakers to pronounce and is designed to reflect how foreign languages are used by native speakers.

You will be amazed at how confidence in your pronunciation leads to an eagerness to talk to other people in their own language.

Whether you want to learn a new language for travel, education, business, study, or personal enrichment, SAY IT RIGHT phrase books offer a simple and effective method of pronunciation and communication.

PRONUNCIATION GUIDE

B@-J㉎NG

Most English speakers are familiar with the Chinese word **Běijīng**. This is how the correct pronunciation is represented in the EPLS Vowel Symbol System.

All Chinese vowel sounds are assigned a specific non-changing symbol. When these symbols are used in conjunction with consonants and read normally, pronunciation of even the most difficult foreign word becomes incredibly EASY!

On the following page are all the EPLS Vowel Symbols used in this book. They are EASY to LEARN since their sounds are familiar. Beneath each symbol are three English words which contain the sound of the symbol.

Practice pronouncing the words under each symbol until you mentally associate the correct vowel sound with the correct symbol. Most symbols are pronounced the way they look!

THE SAME BASIC SYMBOLS ARE USED IN ALL SAY IT RIGHT PHRASE BOOKS!

EPLS VOWEL SYMBOL SYSTEM

Ⓐ
Ace
Bake
Safe

ⒺⒺ
See
Feet
Meet

Ⓘ
Ice
Kite
Pie

Ⓞ
Oak
Cold
Sold

ⓞⓞ
Cool
Pool
Too

ⓔ̆
Men
Red
Bed

ⓐⓗ
Calm
Hot
Off

ⓤⓗ
Up
Sun
Cup

Ⓤⓡ
Hurt
Turn
Her

ⓞⓤ
Would
Could
Cook

ⓞⓦ
Cow
Now
How

ⓔⓦ*
Few
New
Dew

*This symbol represents a sound similar to the French **u**. Put your lips together as if to kiss and say **EE**.

When two symbols appear side by side try to pronounce them as one sound as in the English word "Meow."

TONES

The word **Ma** in Mandarin sounds exactly as in English but has several meanings depending on whether or not the vowel sound rises or falls in pronunciation. The **four** main tones of Mandarin are a **very** important part of the Chinese language and the **EPLS** Vowel Symbol System makes them easy to master!

— **First tone:** A **high** tone reflects a high pitch. The EPLS symbol sits above the syllable to visually illustrate this.

Mother
Mā
M@

↗ **Second tone: Rising** tone is reflected in mid to high pitch as in asking "what?" in Engish. This symbol tilts upward to reflect this tone.

Hemp
Má
M@

∨ **Third tone:*** The only tone which goes in two directions. It **starts downward** to the low range then rises. This symbol is placed below the baseline and tilts upwards.

Horse
Mǎ
M@

↘ **Fourth tone:** The **falling** tone is similar to saying "Stop!" in a commanding way. The symbol simply tilts downward.

Scold
Mà
M@

*There are two very important variations to the third tone as well as a neutral tone. These will be explained on page 3. Have a Chinese-speaking person pronounce some words for you and listen to the variations in sound.

EPLS CONSONANTS

Consonants are letters like **T**, **D**, and **K**. They are easy to recognize and their pronunciation seldom changes. The following pronunciation guide letters represent some unique Chinese consonant sounds.

TS Pronounce these **EPLS** letters like the **ts** in hi**ts** There is a slight puff of air after the **s**. Say wha**t's h**appening and try to get a sense of the slight aspiration before the **h**. Very subtle but much appreciated by native Chinese speakers.

DS Pronounce these **EPLS** letters like the **ds** in su**ds**.

ZH Pronounce these **EPLS** letters like **s** in mea**s**ure.

<u>R</u> The Chinese **r** has no exact equivalent in English. You must hear it and try to duplicate the unique sound.

WHAT IS PINYIN? Mandarin Chinese is represented in this book in both Chinese characters and Pīnyīn. Pīnyīn is a romanized phonetic system officially adopted in China. Although Pīnyīn uses many letters that you are familiar with, unfortunately they often vary wildly in actual Chinese pronunciation. Virtually everyone in China can read characters so we have added this feature as an additional tool allowing you to point to what you are trying to communicate.

ICONS USED IN
THIS BOOK

 ## KEY WORDS

You will find this icon at the beginning of chapters indicating key words relating to chapter content. These are important words to become familiar with.

 ## PHRASEMAKER

The Phrasemaker icon provides the traveler with a choice of phrases that allows the user to make his or her own sentences.

Say It
Right in
CHINESE

ESSENTIAL WORDS AND PHRASES

Here are some basic words and phrases that will help you express your needs and feelings in **Chinese**.

Hello

Nǐ hǎo!   你好

N**EE** H**OW**

How are you?

Nǐ hǎo ma?   你好吗？

N**EE** H**OW** M**ah**

Very good, thanks.

Hěn hǎo, Xiè xie.   很好，谢谢

H**uh**N H**OW** SH**EE**è SH**EE**è

Ok / So so

Mǎmǎ Hūhū.   马马虎虎

M**ah**-M**ah** H**OO**-H**OO**

Literally: Horse Horse Tiger Tiger

And you?

Nǐ ne?   你呢？

N**EE** N**uh**

2

Good morning.

Zǎo shàng hǎo. 早上好

DS⊚w SH⊚NG H⊚w

Good afternoon.

Xiàwǔ hǎo. 下午好

SH⊞⊚-W⊚ H⊚w

Good evening.

Wǎn shàng hǎo. 晚上好

W⊚N-SH⊚NG H⊚w

Good night.

Wǎn ān 晚安

W⊚N-⊚N

See you later.

Yí hui'er jiàn. 一会儿见

⊞ H⊚⊚R J⊞⊚N

Good-bye.

Zài jiàn. 再见

DS⊘ J⊞⊚N

Third tone variations: 1. Notice in the Pīnyīn phrase "Nǐ hǎo" there are two third tones in a row. In actual pronunciation the first tone becomes a **second** or **rising tone**. By following the vowel symbol **which tilts upward** you will do this naturally!

2. A third tone followed by any other tone including a **neutral tone*** becomes a **low tone** or 1/2 third Chinese tone. The vowel symbol sits below the base line but does not tilt up. This is by far the easiest tone to master. Just think **low**.

*Neutral tones: A neutral tone means exactly that. You pronounce it with little emphasis and evenly. The EPLS symbol sits on the baseline and **does not tilt** in any direction.

Yes

Shì   是

SH⬤

Shì almost rhymes with sure but really only has the sh and the r sounds.

No

Bú shì   不是

B⬤   SH⬤

OK

Hǎo   好

H⬤

Please

Qǐng   请

CH⬤NG

Thank you

Xiè xie ni   谢谢你

SH⬤⬤   SH⬤⬤   N⬤

You're welcome

Bú xiè   不谢

B⬤   SH⬤⬤

I'm sorry

Duìbùqǐ   对不起

D⬤⬤-B⬤   CH⬤

This simple way of saying **I'm sorry** can be used in several situations such as when you want to ask a question or when you are trying to get through a crowd!

I don't understand! (literally: I not understand)

Wǒ bù dǒng.   我不懂

W(ah) B(oo) D(o)NG

Do you understand?

Nǐ tīng dé dǒng ma?   你听得懂吗?

N(EE) T(EE)NG D(uh)
D(o)NG M(ah)

I'm a tourist.

Wǒ shì yí gè yóu kè.   我是一个游客

W(ah)-SH(ir) (EE)-G(uh) Y(O)-K(uh)

I don't understand Chinese.

Wǒ bù dǒng hàn yǔ.   我不懂汉语

W(ah) B(oo) D(o)NG
H(an)N Y(ew)

Do you speak English?

Nǐ huì jiǎng yīng yǔ ma?   你会讲英语吗

N(EE) H(oo)(A) J(EE)(ah)NG
Y(EE)NG Y(oo) M(ah)

Please repeat.

Qǐng nǐ zài shuō yí biàn.   请你再说一遍

CH(E)NG N(EE) DS(I)
SH(oo)(ah) (EE)-B(EE)(E)N

FEELINGS

I would like...

Wǒ xiǎng yào...   我想要

W⒜ SH⒠⒜NG Y⒪⒲...

I want...

Wǒ yào...   我要

W⒜ Y⒪⒲...

I have...

Wǒ yǒu...   我有

W⒜ Y⒪...

I know.	**I don't know.**
Wǒ zhī dào. 我知道	Wǒ bù zhī dào. 我不知道
W⒜ J⒰ D⒪⒲	W⒜ B⒪ J⒰ D⒪⒲

I like it.

Wǒ xǐ huān.   我喜欢

W⒜ SH⒠ H⒪⒪⒜N

I don't like it.

Wǒ bù xǐ huān.   我不喜欢

W⒜ B⒪ SH⒠ H⒪⒪⒜N

I'm lost.

Wǒ mí lù le. 我迷路了

W(ah) M(ee)-L(oo) L(uh)

We are lost.

Wǒ men mílù le. 我们迷路了

W(ah)-M(uh)N M(ee)-L(oo) L(uh)

I'm tired.

Wǒ lèi le. 我累了

W(ah) L(a) L(uh)

I'm ill.

Wǒ shēng bìng le. 我生病了

W(ah) SH(uh)NG B(ee)NG L(uh)

I'm hungry.

Wǒ è le. 我饿了

W(ah) (uh) L(uh)

I'm thirsty.

Wǒ kě le. 我渴了

W(ah) K(ou) L(uh)

I'm happy.

Wǒ gāo xìng. 我高兴

W(ah) G(ow) SH(ee)NG

INTRODUCTIONS

Use the following phrases when meeting someone for the first time, both privately and in business. Note that **Nín hǎo** is the polite form of hello.

Hello

Nǐ hǎo   你好   Nín hǎo   您好

N**EE** H**OW**   N**EE**N H**OW**

My name is...

Wǒ jiào... 我叫

W**ah** J**EE****OW**... (your name)

Very nice to meet you. *Glad to meet you too*
Very nice

Hěn gāo xìng rèn shi nǐ!   很高兴认识你   *Wo ye hen gaoxing*

H**uh**N G**OW** SH**EE**NG
R**uh**N SH**Ur** N**EE**

我也很
高兴。

GENERAL GUIDELINES

China is the most populous country on earth and is bound by strict rules and courtesy among its people.

- Mianzi (Face) describes shame in Chinese culture. Do not cause shame by insult, embarrassment, yelling, or talking down to a person.

- Guanxi (Relationships) describes the importance placed on having good people-to-people relationships. This is regarded as a sense of personal best as well as a representation of one's influential power.

- Keqi means considerate, polite, and well mannered.

- It is not wise to show public displays of affection, hand waving, and gestures.

NO VERB CONJUGATIONS

The easiest part of learning Chinese is that there are no verb conjugations. **I, you, he, she, it, we,** and **they**, all take the same verb form.

The verb **"to be"** is **shì**. Notice how its form does not change. This holds true for all Chinese verbs!

I am.

Wǒ **shì.**   我是

W⒜ SH⓾

We are.

Wǒmen **shì.**   我们是

W⒜-M⒨N SH⓾

You are.

Nǐ **shì.**   你是

N⒠ SH⓾

You are. (a group)

Nǐmen **shì.**   你们是

N⒠-M⒨N SH⓾

He / she / it is.

Tā **shì.**   他 / 她 / 它是

T⒜ SH⓾

They are.

Tāmen **shì.**   他们是 / 她们是 / 它们是

T⒜-M⒰N SH⓾

NEGATIVES

A simple way to form a negative in Chinese is to add **bu** (not) in front of the verb.

I eat.	**I don't eat.**
Wǒ chī 我吃	Wǒ **bù** chī 我不吃
Wah CHU	Wah BOO CHU
I want.	**I don't want.**
Wǒ yào 我要	Wǒ **bù** yào 我不要
Wah Yow	Wah BOO Yow
I understand.	**I don't understand.**
Wǒ dǒng 我懂	Wǒ **bù** dǒng 我不懂
Wah DONG	Wah BOO DONG

A notable execption to the above pattern is the verb **"to have"** which takes the word **méi** before it to say **I don't have.**

I have.	**I don't have.**
Wǒ yǒu. 我有	Wǒ **méi** yǒu. 我没有
Wah YO	Wah MA YO

THE BIG QUESTIONS

Who?

Shuí?   谁?

SH︎ⓄⒶ

Who is it?

Tā shì shuí?   他是谁?

Tⓐⓗ   SHⓊ   SHⓄⒶ

What?

Shénme?   什么?

SHⓊN-Mⓤⓗ

What is this?

Zhè shì shénme?   这是什么?

Jⓤⓗ   SHⓊ   SHⓊN-Mⓤⓗ

When?

Shénme shíhòu?   什么时候?

SHⓊN-Mⓤⓗ   SHⓊ-HⓄ

Where?

Nǎ li?   哪里?

Nⓐⓗ   LⒺⒺ

Where is…?

…zài nǎ li?   在哪里?

…DSⓩ Nⓐh LⒺⒺ

Which?

Nǎ yí gè?   哪一个?

Nⓐh ⒺⒺ Gⓞⓤ

Why?

Wèi shénme?   为什么?

Wⓐ SHⓤⓝN-Mⓤh

How?

Zěnme?   怎么?

DSⓤⓗN Mⓤh

How much? (money)

Duōshǎo qián?   多少 (钱)?

Dⓞⓞⓐh-SHⓞw CHⒺⒺⓔN

How long?

Duō cháng shí jiān?   多长时间?

Dⓞⓞⓐh CHⓐNG SHⓤ JⒺⒺⓔN

ASKING FOR THINGS

The following phrases are valuable for directions, food, help, etc.

I would like...

Wǒ xiǎng yào...　我想要

W**ah** SH**EE**a**h**NG Y**ow**...

I need...	**Can you...**
Wǒ xū yào...　我需要	Nǐ néng...　你能
W**ah** SH**oo**-Y**ow**...	N**EE** N**uh**NG...

When asking a question it is polite to say <u>May I ask</u> and <u>Thank you</u>.

May I ask?

Qǐng wèn?　请问？

CH**uh**NG W**uh**

Thank you.

Xièxie nǐ.　谢谢你

SH**EE**e̯ SH**EE**e̯ N**EE**

PHRASEMAKER

Combine I **would like** with the following phrases, and you will have an effective way to ask for things.

I would like...

Wǒ xiǎng yào... 我想要

W@ SH@@NG Y@w...

▶ **coffee**

kāfēi 咖啡

K@-F@

▶ **some water**

shuǐ 水

SH@@@

▶ **ice water**

bīng shuǐ 冰水

B@NG SH@@@

▶ **the menu**

càidān 菜单

TS@-D@N

PHRASEMAKER

Here are a few sentences you can use when you feel the urge to say **I need**... or **can you**...?

I need...

Wǒ xū yào...   我需要

W(ah) SH(oo) Y(ow)...

▶ **your help**

nǐ bāng máng   你帮忙

N(ee) B(ah)NG M(ah)NG

▶ **more money**

gèng duō qián   更多钱

G(uh)NG D(O) CH(ee)(uh)N

▶ **change**

língqián   零钱

L(ee)NG-CH(ee)(uh)N

▶ **a doctor**

yī shēng   医生

(ee) SH(uh)NG

▶ **a lawyer**

lùshī   律师

L(ew)-SH(ur)

PHRASEMAKER

Can you…

Nǐ néng…   你能

N⒠ N⒲NG…

▸ **help me?**

bāng wǒ ma?   帮我吗？

B⒜NG W⒜ M⒜

▸ **give me?**

gěi wǒ ma?   给我吗？

G⒜ W⒜ M⒜

▸ **tell me…?**

gào sù wǒ ma?   告诉我吗？

G⒲-S⒪ W⒜ M⒜

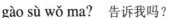

▸ **take me to…?**

dài wǒ qù…?   带我去？

D⒤ W⒜ CH⒪…

ASKING THE WAY

No matter how independent you are, sooner or later you'll probably have to ask for directions.

Where is…?

…zài nǎ li?   在哪里?

…DSⓄ Nⓐ Lⓔⓔ

I'm looking for…

Wǒ zài zhǎo…   我在找

Wⓐ DSⓄ Jⓞⓦ

Is it near?

Jìn ma?   近吗?

JⓔⓔN Mⓐ

Is it far?

Yuǎn ma?   远吗?

YⓞⓞⓐN Mⓐ

I'm lost!

Wǒ mí lù le!   我迷路了!

Wⓐ Mⓔⓔ Lⓞⓞ Lⓤ

PHRASEMAKER

▸ **Restroom...**

Xǐ shǒu jiān...   洗手间

SH㊤ SH⓪ J㊤㊤N...

▸ **Telephone...**

Diànhuà...   电话

D㊤㊤N H⓪⓪㋐...

▸ **Beach...**

Hǎitān...   海滩

H① T㋐N...

▸ **Hotel..**

Lǚguǎn...   旅馆

L㊤ G⓪⓪㋐N...

▸ **The train for...**

Huǒ chē...   火车

H⓪⓪㋐ CH⓪...

...where is it?

...zài nǎ li?   在哪里?

...DS① N㋐ L㊤㊤

TIME

What time is it?

Xiànzài jǐdiǎn?　现在几点？

SHEEⓐN DSⓘ JEE DEEⓐN

Morning

Zǎo shàng　早上

DSⓞⓦ SHⓐNG

Noon

Zhōngwǔ　中午

JⓄNG Wⓞⓞ

Night

Wǎn shàng　晚上

Wⓐ hN SHⓐNG

Today

Jīntiān　今天

JEEN TEEⓔN

Tomorrow

Míngtiān　明天

MⓔNG TEEⓔN

This week

Zhè gè xīngqī   这个星期

J@ G@ SH@NG CH@

This month

Zhè gè yuè   这个月

J@ G@ Y@@

This year

Jīn nián   今年

J@N N@@N

Now

Xiàn zài   现在

SH@@N DS@

Soon

Hěn kuài   很快

H@N K@@

Later

Yì huǐ 'er   一会儿

@ H@@@R

Never

Cóng lái bú huì   从来不会

TS@NG L@ B@ H@@

WHO IS IT?

I

Wǒ   我

W

You

Nǐ   你

N

He / she / it

Tā   他（她，它）

T

We

Wǒmén   我们

W-M

You (plural)

Nǐmen   你们

N-M

They

Tāmen   他们（她们，它们）

T-M

THIS AND THAT

The equivalents of **this, that, these,** and **which** are as follows:

This

Zhè   这

J@

This is mine.

Zhè shì wǒde   这是我的

J@ SH@ W@-D@

That

Nà   那

N@

That is mine.

Nà shì wǒde.   那是我的

N@ SH@ W@-D@

These

Zhè xiē   这些

J@ SH@@

These are mine.

Zhè xiē shì wǒde.   这些是我的

J@ SH@@ SH@ W@-D@

USEFUL OPPOSITES

Near	**Far**
Jìn 近	Yuǎn 远
J◉N	Y◎◉N
Here	**There**
Zhè li 这里	Nà li 那里
J◉-L◉	N◉-L◉
Left	**Right**
Zuǒ biān 左边	Yòu biān 右边
DS◎◉-B◉◉N	Y◎-B◉◉N
A little	**A lot**
Yì diǎn 一点	Hěn duō 很多
◉ D◉◉N	H◉N D◎◉
More	**Less**
Gèng duō 更多	Gèng shǎo 更少
G◉NG D◎◉	G◉NG SH◉
Big	**Small**
Dà 大	Xiǎo 小
D◉	SH◉◉

Open

Kāi　开

K①

Closed

Guān　关

G⓿⓿N

Cheap

Pián yi　便宜

P⓿⓿N Y⓿

Expensive

Guì　贵

G⓿⓿

Clean

Gān jìng　干净

G⓿N J⓿NG

Dirty

Zāng　脏

DS⓿NG

Good

Hǎo　好

H⓿

Bad

Huài　坏

H⓿①

Vacant

Méi rén yòng　没人用

M⓿ R⓿N YONG

Occupied

Yǒu rén yòng　有人用

Y⓿ R⓿N YONG

Right

duì　对

D⓿①

Wrong

cuò　错

TS⓿⓿

WORDS OF ENDEARMENT

I like you.

Wǒ xǐ huān nǐ.   我喜欢你

Wah SHEE HOOahN NEE

I love you.

Wǒ ài nǐ.   我爱你

Wah Ⓘ NEE

I love China.

Wǒ ài zhōngguó.   我爱中国

Wah Ⓘ JONG-GOOah

I love Beijing.

Wǒ ài běijīng.   我爱北京

Wah Ⓘ BA-JEENG

I love Shanghai.

Wǒ ài shànghǎi.   我爱上海

Wah Ⓘ SHahNG-HⒾ

I love Hong Kong.

Wǒ ài xiānggǎng.   我爱香港

Wah Ⓘ SHEEahNG GahNG

WORDS OF ANGER

Go away!

Zǒu kāi!　走开！

DSO KI

Stop bothering me!

Bié fán wǒ!　别烦我！

BEE FAN Wa

What do you want?

Nǐ xiǎng yào shén me?　你想要什么？

NEE SHEEaNG YOW SHuN-Muh

Be quiet!

Ān jìng!　安静！

aN JuNG

That's enough!

Gòu lé!　够了！

GO Luh

COMMON EXPRESSIONS

When you are at a loss for words but have the feeling you should say something, try one of these!

No problem.

Méi wèntí!   没问题

M**Ⓐ** W**ⓤ**N-T**ⓔⓔ**

Congratulations!

Gōng xǐ!   恭喜

G**Ⓞ**NG SH**ⓔⓔ**

Good fortune!

Gōng xǐ fā cái!   恭喜发财

G**Ⓞ**NG SH**ⓔⓔ** F**ⓐⓗ**-TS**Ⓘ**

Welcome!

Huānyíng!   欢迎

H**ⓞⓞⓐⓗ**N-Y**ⓔⓔ**NG

Cheers!

Gān bēi!   干杯！

G**ⓐⓗ**N B**Ⓐ**

Good luck!

Zhù nǐ hǎo yùn!   祝你好运

J㏈ N㏈ H㏒ Y㏈N

My goodness!

Tiān a!   天啊！

T㏈㋐N ㋐

What a shame! / That's too bad.

Hěn zāo gāo.   很糟糕

H㋐N DS㏒ G㏒

Wonderful! Fantastic!

Tài hǎo le!   太好了

T㋛ H㏒ L㋐

USEFUL COMMANDS

Stop!

Tíng! 停

T@NG

Go!

Zǒu ba! 走吧！

DS◎ B@h

Wait!

Děng yí xià! 等一下！

D@NG ⓔ SH@@@

Hurry!

Kuài diǎn! 快点

K@@ⓘ D@@@N

Slow down!

Màn diǎn! 慢点！

M@N D@@@N

Come here!

Dào zhè lái! 到这来！

D@ J@ L①

EMERGENCIES

Fire!

Zháo hǔo le!   着火了！

J⃝ow H⃝oo⃝an L⃝uh

Help!

Jiù mìng!   救命！

J⃝ee⃝oo NG M⃝e⃝o NG

Emergency!

Jǐn jí qíng kuàng!   紧急情况！

J⃝ee N-J⃝ee CH⃝e⃝ong K⃝oo⃝an NG

Call the police!

Jiào jǐng chá!   叫警察！

J⃝ee⃝ow J⃝ee NG-CH⃝an

Call a doctor!

Jiào yī shēng!   叫医生！

J⃝ee⃝ow ⃝ee SH⃝uh NG

Call an ambulance!

Jiào jiù hù chē!   叫救护车！

J⃝ee⃝ow J⃝ee⃝oo H⃝oo-CH⃝uh

ARRIVAL

Passing through customs should be easy since there are usually agents available who speak English. You may be asked how long you intend to stay and if you have anything to declare.

- Have your passport ready.

- Be sure all documents are up-to-date.

- Chinese law is strict and items such as videotaping equipment or movie cameras should be declared upon entry.

- Time used throughout China is Beijing standard time, which is thirteen hours ahead of New York.

- While in a foreign country, it is wise to keep receipts for everything you buy.

- Be aware that many countries will charge a departure tax when you leave. Your travel agent should be able to find out if this affects you.

- If you have connecting flights, be sure to reconfirm them in advance.

- Make sure your luggage is clearly marked inside and out and always keep an eye on it when in public places.

- Take valuables and medicines in carry-on bags.

KEY WORDS

Baggage

Xínglǐ 行李

SH**EE**NG L**EE**

Customs

Hǎi guān 海关

H**I** G**ooah**N

Documents

Wén jiàn 文件

W**uh**N J**EEe**N

Passport

Hù zhào 护照

H**oo** J**ow**

Porter

Bān yùn gōng 搬运工

B**ah**N Y**oo**N G**O**NG

Tax

Shuì 税

SH**ooa**

USEFUL PHRASES

Here is my passport.

Zhè shì wǒ de hù zhào.   这是我的护照

J⑩ SH⑪ W⑳ D⑳
H⑳ J⑳

I have nothing to declare.

Wǒ méi yǒu dōng xī yào shēn bào.
我没有东西要申报

W⑳ M⑳-Y⑩ D⑩NG-SH⑯
Y⑳ SH⑩N-B⑳

I'm here on business.

Wǒ shì lái tán shēng yì de.   我是来谈生意的

W⑳ SH⑪ L⑳
T⑳N-SH⑩NG-⑯ D⑳

I'm on vacation.

Wǒ zài dù jià.   我在度假

W⑳ DS⑳ D⑳-J⑯⑳

Is there a problem?

Yǒu wèn tí ma?   有问题吗？

Y⑩ W⑳N-T⑯ M⑳

PHRASEMAKER

I'll be staying…

Wǒ yào zhù...   我要住

W⒜ Y⒴ J⒪...

▸ **one night**

yígè wǎnshàng   一个晚上

Ⓔ-G⒲ W⒜N-SH⒜NG

▸ **two nights**

liǎng gè wǎnshàng   两个晚上

LⒺ⒜NG-G⒲ W⒜N-SH⒜NG

▸ **one week**

yígè xīngqī   一个星期

Ⓔ-G⒲ SHⒺNG-CHⒺ

▸ **two weeks**

liǎnggè xīngqī   两个星期

LⒺ⒜NG-G⒲ SHⒺNG-CHⒺ

USEFUL PHRASES

I need a porter.

Wǒ yào yí gè bān yùn gōng.

我要一个搬运工

Wah Yow EE-Guh
BaN-YoN-GoNG

These are my bags.

Zhè xiē shì wǒ de bāo.   这些是我的包

ZHuh   SHEEē   SHur
Wah   Duh   Bow

I'm missing a bag.

Wǒ diū le yí gè bāo.   我丢了一个包

Wah   DEEoo   Luh
EE-Guh   Bow

Thank you. This is for you.

Xìe xie. Zhè shì gěi nǐ de.   谢谢。这是给你的。

SHEEē   SHEEē
Juh   SHur   GA   NEE   Duh

PHRASEMAKER

To say **Where is...?**, name
what you are looking for then
go to bottom of the page and say...**zài nǎ lǐ?**

▸ **Customs...**

Hǎi guān...   海关

HⒾ GⓄⓄⓐⓗN...

▸ **Baggage claim...**

Rèn lǐng xíng lǐ...   认领行李

RⓌN LⒺⒺNG SHⒺNG LⒺⒺ...

▸ **The money exchange...**

Wài bì duì huà...   外币兑换

WⒾ BⒺⒺ DⓄⓄⒶ HⓄⓄⓐⓗ...

▸ **The taxi stand...**

Chū zū chē...   出租车

CHⓄⓄ DSⓄⓄ CHⓊⓗ...

▸ **The bus stop...**

Gōng gòng qì chē zhàn...   公共汽车站

GⓄNG-GⓄNG CHⒺⒺ CHⓊⓗ JⓐⓝN...

...where is?

...zài nǎ li?   在哪里？

...DSⒾ Nⓐⓗ LⒺⒺ

HOTEL SURVIVAL

A wide selection of accommodations is available in major cities. The most complete range of facilities is found in five star hotels.

- Make reservations well in advance and request the address of the hotel to be written in Chinese as most taxi drivers do not speak English.

- Faxing is the best way to make your reservations and is customary in China.

- Do not leave valuables or cash in your room when you are not there!

- Electrical items like blow-dryers may need an adapter and/or connector. Your hotel may be able to provide one, but to be safe, take one with you.

- It is a good idea to make sure you give your room number to persons you expect to call you. This can avoid confusion with western names.

- Your hotel front desk can usually assist you with posting mail or packages and many tourist hotels have their own post offices and shipping services.

KEY WORDS

Hotel
Lǚ guǎn 旅馆
L G⑩@N

Bellman
Xǐng lǐ yuán 行李员
SH◉NG L⒠ Y⑩@N

Maid
Fú wù yuán 服务员
F⑩ W⑳ Y⑩@N

Message
Duǎn xìn 短信
D⑩@N SH◉N

Reservation
Yù dìng 预定
Y⑳ D◉NG

Room service
Kè fáng fú wù 客房服务
K⑳ F@NG F⑩ W⑳

CHECKING IN

✓ **My name is…**

Wǒ jiào...   我叫

W@ah J@EE@w...

I have a reservation.

Wǒ yǐ jīng yù dìng le.   我已经预定了

W@ah-EE J@EENG
Y@oo D@ING L@uh

Have you any vacancies?

Yǒu méi yǒu kòng fáng?   有没有空房?

Y@O M@A Y@O
K@ONG F@aNG

What is the charge per night?

Fáng fèi yì tiān dōu shǎo qián?   房费一天多少钱?

F@aNG F@A @EE
T@EE@N D@O SH@ow CH@EE@N

Is there room service?

Yǒu méi yǒu kè fáng fú wù?   有没有客房服务?

Y@O M@A Y@O
K@uh F@aNG F@oo W@oo

PHRASEMAKER

I would like a room with…

Wǒ xiǎng yào yǒu …   我想要有

W⊛ SH㏄⊛NG Y⊛ Y◎…

▸ **a bath**

xǐ shǒu jiān de fángjiān   洗手间 的房间

SH㏄ SH◎ J㏄ⓔN
D⓾ F⊛NG J㏄ⓔN

▸ **one bed**

yì zhāng chuáng de fángjiān   一张床的房间

㏄ J⊛NG CH⊛NG
D⓾ F⊛NG J㏄ⓔN

▸ **two beds**

liǎng zhāng chuáng de fángjiān
两张床的房间

L㏄⊛NG J⊛NG CH⊛NG
D⓾ F⊛NG J㏄ⓔN

▸ **a shower**

yù shì de fángjiān   浴室 的房间

Y⊚ SH⓾
D⓾ F⊛NG J㏄ⓔN

USEFUL PHRASES

My room key, please.

Qǐng gěi wǒ fáng jiān yào shi.   请给我房间钥匙

CH﹝NG GⒶ
WⒶh FⒶNG J﹝﹝N
YⒾW SHⓛ

Are there any messages for me?

Yǒu méi yǒu gěi wǒ de liú yán?   有没有给我的留言？

YⒾ MⒶ YⒾ
GⒶ WⒶh Dⓛh L﹝ｸ YⒶN

Where is the dining room?

Cān tīng zài nǎ li?   餐厅在哪里？

TSⒶN T﹝NG DSⓈ NⒶ L﹝

Are meals included?

Bāo kuò cān fèi ma?   包括餐费吗？

BⒾW KⒸⒶh
TSⒶN FⒶ MⒶh

What time is breakfast?

Shén me shí hòu yǒu zǎo cān?
什么时候有早餐？

SHⒶN-Mⓛh SHⓛ-HⒾ
YⒾ DSⒾW TSⒶN

PHRASEMAKER
(WAKE UP CALL)

Please wake me at...

Qǐng (...) jiào xǐng wǒ. 请叫醒我

CHⒺNG (...) JⒺⓄⓌ SHⒺNG WⓐH

▸ **6:00 a.m.**

...zǎo chén liù diǎn... 早晨六点

...DSⓄⓌ CHⓊN LⒺⓄ DⒺⒺN...

▸ **6:30 a.m.**

...zǎo chén liù diǎn bàn... 早晨六点半

...DSⓄⓌ CHⓊN LⒺⓄ DⒺⒺN BⓐN...

▸ **7:00 a.m.**

...zǎo chén qī diǎn... 早晨七点

...DSⓄⓌ CHⓊN CHⒺ DⒺⒺN...

▸ **7:30 a.m.**

...zǎo chén qī diǎn bàn... 早晨七点半

...DSⓄⓌ CHⓊN CHⒺ DⒺⒺN BⓐN...

▸ **8:00 a.m.**

...zǎo chén bā diǎn... 早晨八点

...DSⓄⓌ CHⓊN BⓐH DⒺⒺN...

▸ **9:00 a.m.**

...zǎo chén jǔ diǎn... 早晨九点

...DSⓄⓌ CHⓊN JⓄⓌ DⒺⒺN...

PHRASEMAKER

I need…

Wǒ xūyào...   我需要

W**ah** SH**oo**-Y**ow**…

▶ **a babysitter**

bǎo mǔ   保姆

B**ow** M**oo**

▶ **a bellman**

xíng lǐ yuán   行李员

SH**e**NG L**ee** Y**oo**(**ah**)N

▶ **more blankets**

gèng duō máo tǎn   更多毛毯

G**u**NG D**oo**(**ah**) M**ow** T**ah**N

▶ **a hotel safe**

bǎo xiǎn xiāng   保险箱

B**ow** SH**ee**(**ah**)N SH**ee**(**ah**)NG

▶ **ice cubes**

bīng kuài   冰块

B**ee**NG K**oo**(**i**)

▶ **an extra key**

lìng wài yì bǎ yàoshi   另外一把钥匙

L**ⓔ**NG-W**ⓘ** **ⓔⓔ** B**ⓐⓗ**
Y**ⓞⓦ**-SH**ⓤ**

▶ **a maid**

fú wù yuán   服务员

F**ⓞⓞ** W**ⓞⓞ** Y**ⓞⓞⓐ**N

▶ **the manager**

jīng lǐ   经理

J**ⓔⓔ**NG L**ⓔⓔ**

▶ **clean sheets**

gān jìng de chuáng dān   干净的床单

G**ⓐⓗ**N J**ⓔ**NG D**ⓤⓗ**
CH**ⓞⓞⓐ**NG D**ⓐⓗ**N

▶ **soap**

féi zào   肥皂

F**ⓐ** DS**ⓞⓦ**

▶ **toilet paper**

wèi shēng zhǐ   卫生纸

W**ⓐ** SH**ⓤ**NG J**ⓤ**

▶ **more towels**

gèng duō máo jīn   更多毛巾

G**ⓤ**NG D**ⓞⓞⓐ** M**ⓞⓦ** J**ⓔⓔ**N

PHRASEMAKER

(PROBLEMS)

There is no…

Méi yǒu...　没有

M Ⓐ　YⓄ…

▸ **electricity**

diàn le　电了

DⒺⒺⒶN　LⓊⒽ

▸ **heat**

nuǎn qì le　暖气

NⓄⓄⒶⒽN　CHⒺⒺ　LⓊⒽ

▸ **hot water**

rè shuǐ le　热水了

Ra̲Ⓤ　SHⓄⓄⒶ　LⓊⒽ

▸ **light**

dēng le　灯了

DⓊⒽNG　LⓊⒽ

▸ **toilet paper**

wèi shēng zhǐ le　卫生纸了

WⒶ　SHⓊⒽNG　JⓊⓇ　LⓊⒽ

PHRASEMAKER

(SPECIAL NEEDS)

Do you have…

Nǐ zhè'er yǒu...   你这有

N⒠ J⒲⒜⒝ Y◉...

▶ **an elevator?**

diàn tī ma?   电梯吗？

D⒠⒠N T⒠ M⒜

▶ **a ramp?**

xié pō dào ma?   斜坡道吗？

SH⒠ P◎ D⒪⒲ M⒜

▶ **a wheel chair?**

lún yǐ ma?   轮椅吗？

L⒪⒩N ⒠ M⒜

▶ **facilities for the disabled?**

cán jí rén shè shī ma?   残疾人设施吗？

TS⒜N-J⒠ R⒪N

SH◍ SH⒰ M⒜

CHECKING OUT

The bill, please.

Qǐng gěi wǒ zhàng dān.   请给我账单

CH**Ⓔ**NG G**Ⓐ** W**ⓐ**
J**ⓐ**NG D**ⓐ**N

Is this bill correct?

Zhè zhāng zhàng dān duì ma?   这张账单对吗？

J**ⓤ** J**ⓐ**NG J**ⓐ**NG
D**ⓐ**N D**ⓞⓞⒶ** M**ⓐ**

Do you accept credit cards?

Kéyǐ yòng xìnyòng kǎ ma?   可以用信用卡吗？

K**ⓤ**-Y**Ⓔ** Y**Ⓞ**NG
SH**Ⓔ**N-Y**Ⓞ**NG K**ⓐ** M**ⓐ**

Could you have my luggage brought down?

Néng bāng wǒ bǎ xínglǐ ná xià lái ma?
能帮我把行李拿下来吗？

N**ⓤ**NG B**ⓐ**NG
W**ⓐ** B**ⓐ** SH**Ⓔ**NG-L**Ⓔ**
N**Ⓐ** SH**Ⓔⓐ** L**Ⓘ** M**ⓐ**

Please call a taxi.

Qǐng jiào chūzūchē.　请叫出租车

CHⓔNG Jⓔ(ow)
CH(oo)-DS(oo)-CH(uh)

I had a very good time!

Wǒ zài zhè li guò de hěn yú kuài!　我在这里过得很愉快!

W(ah)　DS(i)　J(uh)
L(ee)　G(oo)(ah)　D(uh)
H(uh)N　Y(oo)　K(oo)(i)

Thanks for everything.

Xiè xie wèi wǒ zuò de yí qiè.　谢谢为我做的一切

SHⓔ(e)　SHⓔ(e)
W(i)　W(ah)　DS(oo)(ah)
D(uh)　ⓔ　CHⓔ(e)

We'll see you next time.

Wǒ men xià cì zài jiàn.　我们下次再见

W(ah)-M(uh)N　SHⓔ(ah)
TS(i)　DS(i)　Jⓔ(e)N

Good-bye

Zài jiàn　再见

DS(i)　Jⓔ(e)N

RESTAURANT SURVIVAL

China boasts one of the world's greatest cuisines and enjoys high marks for color, flavor, and aroma. Chinese food is very popular and you will find a variety of specialties, that are both delicious and inexpensive.

- Beijing breakfast snacks sold by street vendors are worth trying. They consist of vegetables wrapped in an omelette wrapped in a pancake and are called **Jiān bǐng.**

- In many cases some of the least expensive restaurants serve up the tastiest dishes.

- You will not find traditional Chinese meals in western fast-food restaurants.

- Ordering foods is a joint affair and the dishes are served and placed in the center of table for all to enjoy.

- Mineral water in plastic bottles is available in most cities as tap water is not suitable for drinking.

- It is customary for one person to pay the bill as splitting a bill is not done.

- There are no taxes or tipping.

KEY WORDS

Breakfast

Zǎo cān 早餐

DS⊚ TS⒜N

Lunch

Wǔ cān 午餐

W⊚ TS⒜N

Dinner

Wǎn cān 晚餐

W⒜N TS⒜N

Waiter

Fú wù yuán 服务员

F⊚ W⊚ Y⊚⒜N

Waitress

Fú wù yuán 服务员

F⊚ W⊚ Y⊚⒜N

Restaurant

Fàn diàn 饭店

F⒜N D⒠⒠⒠N

USEFUL PHRASES

The menu, please.

Qǐng gěi wǒ cài dān.   请给我菜单

CH**E**NG G**A** W**ah**
TS**O** D**ah**N

Separate checks, please.

Fēn kāi fù zhàng.   分开付帐

F**uh**N K**I** F**oo** J**ah**NG

We are in a hurry.

Wǒ men yǒu jí shì.   我们有急事

W**ah**-M**uh**N Y**O** J**EE** SH**u**

What do you recommend?

Nǐ yǒu shénme kěyǐ tuī jiàn dēma?
你有什么可以推荐的吗？

N**EE** Y**O** SH**O**N-M**uh**
K**uh**-Y**EE** T**ooA**
J**EEO**N D**uh**-M**ah**

Please bring me...

Qǐng gěi wǒ...   请给我

CH®NG G® W®...

Please bring us...

Qǐng gěi wǒmen...   请给我们

CH®NG G® W®-M®N

I'm hungry.

Wǒ è le.   我饿了

W® ® L®

I'm thirsty.

Wǒ kě le.   我渴了

W® K® L®

Is service included?

Bāo kuò fú wù fèi ma?   包括服务费吗？

B®-K®® F® W® F® M®

The bill, please.

Qǐng gěi wǒ zhàng dǎn.   请给我账单

CH®NG G®

W® J®NG D®N

CHINESE CUISINES AND STYLES

The remainder of this chapter will help you order foods you are familiar with. On these pages you will find information on "Dish Systems," customs, and utensils commonly used in China.

Utensils:

Chopsticks are used as tableware in China and are considered to reflect gentleness rather than the knife and fork used in Western civilization.

It is not a good idea to place chopsticks upright in your rice bowl as it is observed as impolite.

Dish Styles:

There are eight "Dish Systems" in China. Each dish system stresses a variety of cooking combinations and entrees with respective oils, sauces, spiciness, tenderness, and crispness features.

Famous Dish Systems:

Three famous cuisines in Chinese cooking are Sichuan, Shandong, and Guangdon (Cantonese) dishes. They vary from Sichuan Dish (hot and tangy) to the Shandong Dish (fresh, crisp, and light).

One very popular dish is Beijing Roast Duck. As with other dishes from the Beijing area, it has its roots in many hundreds of years of Chinese cooking. This delectable dish is one not to be missed!

Cantonese cuisine is one of the four main cuisines in China and encompasses crisp, tender and quick-fried dishes, such as Shark's Fin and Bird's Nest.

Beverage:

Tea (cha) is the most popular drink in China. Make sure the spout is facing out from the table.

BEVERAGE LIST

Coffee
Kā fēi   咖啡

K⒜-F⒜

Decaffeinated coffee
Wú kā fēi yīn kā fēi   无咖啡因咖啡

W⓪ K⒜-F⒜ ⒠N K⒜-F⒜

Cream
Năi yóu   奶油

N① Y◎

Sugar
Táng de   糖

T⒜NG

Tea
Chá   茶

CH⒜

Ice
Bīng   冰

B⒠NG

Lemon
Níng méng   柠檬

N⒠NG M⒠NG

Milk

Níu nǎi   牛奶

NEE⊚ N①

Hot chocolate

Rè qiǎo kè lì   热巧克力

Ru CHEEow Kuh LEE

Juice

Guǒ zhī   果汁

Gooah JUr

Orange juice

Chéng zhī   橙汁

CHuNG JUr

Ice water

Bīng shuǐ   冰水

BEENG SHooA

Mineral water

Kuàng quán shuǐ   矿泉水

Kooahng Kooahn SHooA

AT THE BAR

Bartender

Jiǔ bā zhāo dài　酒吧招待

J㏊-B㏊　J㏊　D⊘

The wine list, please.

Qíng gěi wǒ jiǔdān　请给我酒单

CH㏊NG　G㊀　W㏊　J㏊-D㏊N

Cocktail

Jī wěi jiǔ　鸡尾酒

J㏊　W㊀　J㏊

On the rocks

Jiǎ bīng de　加冰的

J㏊　B㏊NG　D㏊

Straight

Bù jiā bīng de　不加冰的

B㏊　J㏊　B㏊NG　D㏊

With lemon

Jiā níng méng　加柠檬

J㏊　N㏊NG　M㏊NG

PHRASEMAKER

I would like a glass of…

Qǐng gěi wǒ yī bēi...   请给我一杯

CH**EE**NG G**A** W**ah** **EE** B**A**…

▶ **champagne**

xiāng bīn   香槟

SH**EE**ah**NG B**EE**N

▶ **beer**

pí jiǔ   啤酒

P**EE** J**EE**O

▶ **wine**

pú táo jiǔ   葡萄酒

P**oo** T**ow** J**EE**O

▶ **red wine**

hóng pú táo jiǔ   红葡萄酒

H**O**NG P**oo** T**ow** J**EE**O

▶ **white wine**

bái pú táo jiǔ   白葡萄酒

B**I** P**oo** T**ow** J**EE**O

FAMILIAR FOODS

On the following pages you will
find lists of foods you are familiar
with, along with other information
such as basic utensils and preparation
instructions.

A polite way to get a waiter's or waitress's
attention is to say **Má fán ni?**, which means **May
I ask,** followed by your request and thank you.

Excuse me?

Má fán ni?   麻烦你？

M@-F@N N€€

Please bring me...

Qǐng gěi wǒ...   请给我

CH€NG G@ W@....

Thank you.

Xiè xie ni.   谢谢你

SH€€€ SH€€€ N€€

STARTERS

Appetizers

Kāi wèi cài   开胃菜

K① W④ TS②

Bread and butter

Miàn bāo hé huáng yóu   面包和黄油

MⒺⒺⒼN BⓄⓌ HⓊN HⓄⓄⒶNG YⓄ

Cheese

Nǎi lào   奶酪

N① LⓄⓌ

Fruit

Shuǐ guǒ   水果

SHⓄⓄⒶ GⓄⓄⒶⓃ

Salad

Sè lā   色拉

SⓊ LⒶⒽ

Soup

Tāng   汤

TⒶⒽNG

MEAT

Bacon

Xūn ròu   熏肉

SH⊕⊕N Ḇ⦰

Beef

Niú ròu   牛肉

N⦅EE⦆⊕⊕ Ḇ⦰

Beef steak

Niú pái   牛排

N⦅EE⦆⊕⊕ P⦅①⦆

Ham

Huǒ tuǐ   火腿

H⊕⊕⦅ah⦆ T⊕⊕⦅A⦆

Lamb

Yáng ròu   羊肉

Y⦅ah⦆NG Ḇ⦰

Pork

Zhū ròu   猪肉

J⊕⊕ Ḇ⦰

Veal

Nèn niú ròu   嫩牛肉

N⦅ah⦆N N⦅EE⦆⊕⊕ Ḇ⦰

POULTRY

Baked chicken

Kǎo jī 烤鸡

Broiled chicken

Shāo jī 烧鸡

Fried chicken

Zhá jī 炸鸡

Duck

Yā zi (ròu) 鸭子（肉）

Goose

É (ròu) 鹅（肉）

Turkey

Huǒ jī (ròu) 火鸡（肉）

SEAFOOD

Fish

Yú   鱼

Y◎◎

Lobster

Lóng xiā   龙虾

L◎NG   SH㉱㉱ⓐⓗ

Oysters

Háo   蚝 / mǔ lì   牡蛎

H◎ⓦ   /   M◎◎-L㉱㉱

Salmon

Sān wén yú   三文鱼

SⓐⓗN   WⓤⓗN   Y◎◎

Shrimp

Xiā   虾

SH㉱㉱ⓐⓗ

Trout

Guì yú   鲑鱼

G◎◎㉱ⓐ   Y◎◎

Tuna

Jīn qiāng yú   金枪鱼

J㉱N   CH㉱㉱ⓐⓗNG   Y◎◎

OTHER ENTREES

Sandwich

Sān míng zhì   三明治

S@N M@NG J@

Hot dog

Rè gǒu   热狗

R@ G@

Hamburger

Hàn bǎo bāo   汉堡包

H@N B@ B@

French fries

Zhá shǔ tiáo   炸薯条

J@ SH@ T@@

Pasta

Yì dà lì miàn tiáo   意大利面条

Y@ D@ L@ M@@N T@@

Pizza

Bǐ sà   比萨

B@ S@

VEGETABLES

Carrots

Hú luó bo　　胡萝卜

H◎◎　L◎◎◎◎　B◎

Corn

Yù mǐ　　玉米

Y◎◎　M◎◎

Mushrooms

Mó gu　　蘑菇

M◎　G◎◎

Onions

Yáng cōng　　洋葱

Y◎NG　TS◎NG

Potato

Tǔ dòu　　土豆

T◎◎　D◎

Rice

(Dà)　Mǐ　　（大）米

D◎◎　M◎◎

Tomato

Xī hóng shì　　西红柿

SH◎◎　H◎NG　SH◎

FRUITS

Apple
Píng guǒ 苹果

P(EE)NG G(OO)(ah)

Banana
Xiāng jiāo 香蕉

SH(EE)(ah)NG J(EE)(OW)

Grapes
Pú táo 葡萄

P(OO) T(OW)

Lemon
Níng méng 柠檬

N(EE)NG M(UH)NG

Orange
Jú zi 橘子 / Chéng zi 橙子

J(EW)-DZ(uh) / CH(UH)NG DZ(uh)

Strawberry
Cǎo méi 草莓

TS(OW) M(A)

Watermelon
Xī guā 西瓜

SH(EE) G(OO)(ah)

DESSERT

Desserts
Tián diǎn   甜点

T**EE**N D**EE**N

Apple pie
Píng guǒ pài   苹果派

P**E**NG G**OO**N P**I**

Cherry pie
Yīngtáo pài   樱桃派

Y**E**NG-T**OW** P**I**

Pastries
Gāo diǎn   糕点

G**OW** D**EE**N

Candy
Táng   糖

T**A**NG

Ice cream

Bīng ji líng　冰激凌

BEENG JEE LEENG

Ice cream cone

Bīng ji líng dàn juǎn　冰激凌蛋卷

BEENG JEE
LEENG DAN JOOAN

Chocolate

Qiǎo kè lì　巧克力

CHEEow KUH LEE

Strawberry

Cǎo méi　草莓

TSow MA

Vanilla

Xiāng cǎo　香草

SHEEUHNG TSow

CONDIMENTS

Butter

Huáng yóu   黄油

H⓪⓪Ⓐ NG   Y◎

Ketchup

Fān qié jiàng   番茄酱

FⒶN   CHⒺⒺⓉ   JⒺⒺⒶNG

Mayonnaise

Dàn huáng jiàng   蛋黄酱

DⒶN   H⓪⓪ⒶNG   JⒺⒺⒶNG

Mustard

Jiè mò   芥末

JⒺⒺⒶ   M◎

Salt	**Pepper**
Yán 盐	Hú jiāo 胡椒
YⒶN	H⓪⓪ JⒺⒺⓄⓌ

Sugar

Táng   糖

TⒶNG

Vinegar	**Oil**
Cù 醋	Yóu 油
TS⓪⓪	Y◎

SETTINGS

A cup

Yí gè chá bēi 一个茶杯

Ⓔ Ⓖⓤ CHⓐ Ⓑ④

A glass

Yí gè bōli bēi 一个玻璃杯

Ⓔ Ⓖⓤ BⓄ-LⒺ Ⓑ④

A spoon

Yì bǎ sháo zi 一把勺子

Ⓔ Ⓑⓐ SHⓄ DSⓊr

A fork

Yì bǎ chā zi 一把叉子

Ⓔ Ⓑⓐ CHⓐ DSⓊr

A knife

Yì bǎ cān dāo 一把餐刀

Ⓔ Ⓑⓐ TSⓐN DⓄ

A plate

Yí gè pán zi 一个盘子

Ⓔ Ⓖⓤ PⓐN DSⓊr

A napkin

Yī zhāng cān jīn zhǐ 一张餐巾纸

Ⓔ JⓐNG TSⓐN JⒺN JⓊ

HOW DO YOU
WANT IT COOKED?

Baked

Kǎo de   烤的

K**ow** D**uh**

Broiled	**Steamed**
Zhǔ de 煮的	Zhēng de 蒸的
J**oo** D**uh**	J**uh**NG D**uh**

Fried

Zhá de 炸的

J**a** D**uh**

Rare

Shēng yì diǎn de   生一点的

SH**uh**NG **EE** D**EE**N D**uh**

Medium	**Well done**
Zhōng děng de 中等的	Shú de 熟的
J**O**NG D**UH**NG D**uh**	SH**oo** D**uh**

I want to order non-spicy dishes.

Wǒ xiǎng diàn bú là de cài.
我想点不辣的菜

W**a**

PROBLEMS

I didn't order this.

Wǎ méi yǒu yào zhè ge.　我没有要这个。

W⒜h M⒜ Y⒪ Y⒪w J⒰h G⒰h

Is the bill correct?

Zhè zhàng dān duì ma?　这账单对吗？

J⒪ ZH⒜NG D⒜hN D⒪⒪⒜ M⒜h

Bring me…

Qǐng gěi wǒ...　请给我

CH⒠NG G⒜ W⒪...

PRAISE

Thank you for the delicious meal.

Hěn hǎo chī　很好吃

H⒠N H⒪w CH⒠

GETTING AROUND

Getting around in a foreign country can be an adventure in itself! Taxi and bus drivers do not always speak English, so it is essential to be able to give simple directions. The words and phrases in this chapter will help you get where you're going.

- China is considered a safe place to visit and major cities have good transportation including public buses, tour buses, mini buses, and taxis.

- Taxis are always metered. Taxis are fairly cheap and reliable and are the best way to get around.

- Have a map or the address you want to go to written down in Chinese.

- Remember to take a business card from your hotel to give to the taxi driver on your return.

- Train tickets can be booked at your hotel or at the Foreigners' Ticket Office in the Beijing Railway Station and the West Station.

KEY WORDS

Airport

Fēi jī chǎng   飞机场

FⒶ Jⓙ CH⒡NG

Bus Station / Bus Stop

Qì chē zhàn   汽车站

CHⒶⒶ CHⓛ J⒡N

Car Rental Agency

Zū chē chù   租车处

Jⓚ CHⓛ CHⓚ

Subway Station

Dì tiě zhàn   地铁站

DⒶⒶ TⒶⒶⓈ J⒡N

Taxi Stand

Chū zū chē zhàn   出租车站

CHⓚ DSⓚ CHⓛ J⒡N

Train Station

Huǒ chē zhàn   火车站

Hⓚ⒡h CHⓛ J⒡N

AIR TRAVEL

Airport

Fēi jī chǎng   飞机场

F︎Ⓐ JⓊⓇ CHⒶNG

A one-way ticket, please.

Qǐng gěi wǒ yì zhāng dān chéng chē piào.

请给我一张单程车票

CHⒺNG GⓀ WⒶh

ⒺⒺ JⒶhNG DⒶhN

CHⒶNG CHⓊh PⒺⒺⓄw

A round trip ticket.

Shuāng chéng / Wǎng fǎn chē piào.

双程（往返）车票

SHⓄⓄⒶhNG CHⒶNG

WⒶNG FⒶhN CHⓊh PⒺⒺⓄw

First class

Tóu děng cāng   头等舱

TⓄ DⓊhNG TSⒶhN

How much do I owe?

Wǒ yào fù duō shǎo qián?   我要付多少钱?

WⒶh YⓄw FⓄⓄ DⓄⓄⒶh SHⓄw CHⒺⒺⒶN

PHRASEMAKER

I would like a seat...

Wǒ xiǎng yào gè...   我想要个

W**@** SH**©@**NG Y**@** G**@**...

▶ **in first class**

tóu děng cāng de zuò wèi   头等舱的座位

T**©** D**@**NG TS**@**NG D**@**
DS**@@** W**@**

▶ **next to the window**

kào chuāng hù de zuò wèi   靠窗户的座位

K**@** CH**@@**NG H**@** D**@**
DS**@@** W**@**

▶ **on the aisle**

kào guò dào de zuò wèi   靠过道的座位

K**@** G**@@**-D**@** D**@**
DS**@@** W**@**

▶ **near the exit**

kào jìn chū kǒu de zuò wèi   靠近出口的 座位

K**@** J**@**N CH**@** K**©** D**@**
DS**@@** W**@**

BY BUS

Bus

Gōng gòng qì chē   公共汽车

G◉NG G◉NG CH㉫ CH⓾

Where is the bus stop?

Gōng gòng qì chē zhàn zài nǎ li?
公共汽车站在哪里？

G◉NG G◉NG CH㉫ CH⓾
JⓐN DS◯ Nⓐ L㉫

Do you go to…?

Nǐ qù…?   你去

N㉫ CH◎

What is the fare?

Piào jià dūo shǎo?   票价多少？

P㉫◎-J㉫ⓐ D◎ⓐ SH◎

Do I need exact change?

Xū yào zhèng hǎo de líng qián ma?
需要正好的零钱吗？

SH◎ Y◎ JⓐNG
H◎ D⓾ L㉫NG
CH㉫◉N Mⓐ

PHRASEMAKER

Which bus goes to…

Nǎ liàng qì chē qù…   哪辆汽车去

N⒜ L⒠⒠⒡NG CH⒠⒠ CH⒰ CH⒪⒪…

▸ **Tian'anmen square?**

Tiān'ānmēn guǎng chǎng?   天安门广场

T⒠⒠⒜N ⒜N M⒰N
G⒪⒪⒜NG CH⒜NG

▸ **the beach?**

hǎi tān?   海滩

H⒤ T⒜N

▸ **the Forbidden City?**

Gù gōng?   故宫？

G⒪⒪ G⒪NG

BY CAR

Can you help me?

Nǐ néng bāng wǒ ma?   你能帮我吗?

N**ᴇᴇ** N**ᴜ**NG
B**ᴀʜ**NG W**ᴀʜ** M**ᴀʜ**

My car won't start.

Wǒ de chē bù néng kāi le.   我的车不能开了

W**ᴀʜ** D**ᴜʜ** CH**ᴜʜ** B**ᴏᴏ**
N**ᴜ**NG K**ɪ** L**ᴜʜ**

Can you fix it?

Nǐ néng xiū hǎo tā ma?   你能修好它吗?

N**ᴇᴇ** N**ᴜ**NG
SH**ᴇᴇᴏᴏ** H**ᴏw** T**ᴀʜ** M**ᴀʜ**

What will it cost?

Yào duō shǎo qián?   要多少钱?

Y**ᴏw** D**ᴏᴏᴀʜ** SH**ᴏw** J**ᴇᴇᴇ**N

How long will it take?

Yào duō cháng shí jiān?   要多长时间?

Y**ᴏw** D**ᴏᴏᴀʜ** CH**ᴀʜ**NG SH**ᴜ**
J**ᴇᴇᴇ**N SH**ᴜ** J**ᴇᴇᴇ**N

PHRASEMAKER

Please check…

Qǐng jiǎn chá... 请检查

CH**Ĕ**NG J**ĔĔ**N CH**ah**...

▶ **the battery**

diàn chí 电池

D**ĔĔ**N CH**ȕ**

▶ **the brakes**

shā chē 刹车

SH**ah** CH**uh**

▶ **the oil**

jī yóu 机油

J**ĔĔ** Y**O**

▶ **the tires**

lún tāi 轮胎

L**oo**N T**Ĭ**

▶ **the water**

shuǐ xiāng 水箱

SH**ooA** SH**ĔĔah**NG

SUBWAYS AND TRAINS

Where is the train station?

Huǒ chē zhàn zài nǎ li?   火车站在哪里？

H⑩ah CH⑩ J⑩N DS⓪ N⑩ L㋓

A one-way ticket, please.

Qǐng gěi wǒ yì zhāng dān chéng chē piào.

请给我一张单程车票

CH㋐NG G⑩ W⑩

㋓ J⑩NG D⑩N

CH⑩NG CH⑩ P㋓⑩

A round trip ticket.

Shuāng chéng / Wǎng fǎn chē piào.

双程（往返）车票

SH⑩⑩NG CH⑩NG

W⑩NG F⑩N CH⑩ P㋓⑩

First class

Tóu děng cāng   头等舱

T⑥ D⑩NG TS⑩N

Second class

Èr děng cāng   二等舱

⑩R D⑩NG TS⑩NG

What is the fare?

Piào jià duō shǎo?　票价多少？

P㊎㊏　J㊎㊍　D㊏㊍　SH㊏

Is this seat taken?

Zhě ge zuò wèi yǒu rén ma?　这个座位有人吗？

J㊍　G㊎　DS㊏㊍　W㊐
Y㊏　R㊍N　M㊍

Do I have to change trains?

Wǒ bì xū huàn huǒ chē ma?　我必须换火车吗？

W㊍　B㊎　SH㊏　H㊏㊍N
H㊏㊍　CH㊎　M㊍

Where are we?

Wǒ men (xiàn zài) zài nǎ?　我们（现在）在哪？

W㊍-M㊎N　(SH㊎㊍N　DS㊏)
DS㊏　N㊍

BY TAXI

Please call a taxi for me.

Qǐng bāng wǒ jiào liàng chē　请帮我叫辆车

CH㋐NG B㋐NG W㋐ J㋵㋺
L㋵㋐NG CH㋿

Are you available?

Nǐ yǒu kòng mā?　你有空吗？

N㋵ Y㋴ K㋴NG M㋐

I want to go...

Wǒ xiǎng qù...　我想去

W㋐ SH㋵㋐NG CH㋴...

Stop here, please.

Qǐng zài zhè'er tíng yí xià.　请在这儿停一下

CH㋐NG DS㋿ J㋿R
T㋴NG ㋵ SH㋵㋐

Please wait.

Qǐng děng yí huǐ 'er.　请等一会儿

CH㋐NG D㋿NG ㋵ H㋴-㋐R

How much do I owe?

Wǒ yào fù duō shǎo qián?　我要付多少钱？

W㋐ Y㋴ F㋴ D㋴㋐ SH㋴ CH㋵㋐N

PHRASEMAKER

The simplest way to get to
where you want to go is to
name the destination and simply say **please**.

▸ **This address...**

Dì zhǐ ...   地址

D℠ J℠...

Have someone at your hotel write down the address
for you in Chinese characters.

▸ **This hotel...**

Jǔ diàn...   酒店

J℠ D℠N...

▸ **Airport...**

Fēi jī chǎng...   飞机场

F℠ J℠ CH℠NG...

▸ **Subway station...**

Dì tiě zhàn...   地铁站

D℠ T℠ J℠N...

                    ...please.

                    ...qǐng.   请

                    ...CH℠NG

SHOPPING

Whether you plan a major shopping spree or just need to purchase some basic necessities, the following information is useful.

- You can find duty-free shops in airports, major trains stations, and tourist cities.

- Prices are usually cheaper in duty-free shops and you can find money exchange shops here.

- There are also state-run "friendship" stores that carry quality merchandise but less selection.

- Beijing offers a variety of arts and crafts, outdoor markets, and large department stores and bargaining in markets is welcomed.

- Always remember to ask for receipts. You will need to show your passport to the sales assistant when you purchase the goods to allow him or her to fill out the VAT form.

- It's best not to pack your purchases into your check-in luggage.

- At the airport, get your VAT form stamped at the VAT refund desk.

KEY WORDS

Credit card

Xìn yòng kǎ   信用卡

SH**ⓔ**N   Y**Ⓞ**NG   K**ⓐ**h

Money

Qián   钱

CH**ⓔⓔ**N

Receipt

Shōu jù   收据

SH**Ⓞ**   J**ⓞⓞ**

Sale

Dǎ zhé   打折

D**ⓐ**h   J**ⓤ**h

Store

Shāng diàn   商店

SH**ⓐ**NG   D**ⓔⓔ**N

Traveler's checks

Lǚ xíng zhī piào   旅行支票

L**ⓔⓦ**   SH**ⓔ**NG   J**ⓔⓔ**   P**ⓔⓔⓞ**W

USEFUL PHRASES

Do you sell…?

Nǐ mài…?   你卖

N<ee> M<i>…

Do you have…?

Nǐ yǒu…?   你有

N<ee> Y<o>…

I want to buy.

Wǒ xiǎng mǎi.   我想买

W<ah> SH<ee><ah>NG M<i>

How much?

Duō shǎo qián?   多少钱？

D<oo><ah> SH<ow> CH<ee><n>N

When are the shops open?

Shāng diàn shén me shí hòu kāi mén?
商店什么时候开门？

SH<ah>NG D<ee><n>N

SH<n>N-M<uh> SH<ss>-H<o>

K<i> M<n>N

No, thank you.

Bù, xiè xie.   不，谢谢

B⊚⊚ SH⒠⒠⒠ SH⒠⒠⒠

I'm just looking.

Wǒ zhǐ shì kàn kàn.   我只是看看

W⒜ⓗ J⒰ⓡ SH⒰ K⒜ⓗN K⒜ⓗN

Is it very expensive?

Zhè hěn guì ma?   这很贵吗？

J⒰ H⒰ⓗN G⒪⒪⒜ M⒜ⓗ

Can't you give me a discount?

Nǐ kě yǐ gěi wǒ dǎ zhé ma?   你可以给我打折吗？

N⒠⒠ K⒪⒰ ⒠⒠
G⒜ W⒜ⓗ D⒜ⓗ
J⒰ M⒜ⓗ

I'll take it.

Wǒ yào le!   我要了！

W⒜ⓗ Y⒪ⓦ L⒰ⓗ

I'd like a receipt, please.

Qǐng gěi wǒ shōu jù.   请给我收据

CH⒠ⓝNG G⒜ W⒜ⓗ
SH⒪ J⒰

SHOPS AND SERVICES

Bakery

Gāobǐng dìan   糕饼店

G**OW** B**EE**NG D**EE**Ⓔ**N**

### Bank	### Hair salon
Yín háng 银行	Fà láng 发廊
Y**EE**N H**ⓐ**NG	F**ⓐ** L**ⓐ**NG
### Barbershop	### Jewelry store
Lǐfà diàn 理发店	Zhùbǎo diàn 首饰店
L**EE**-F**ⓐ** D**EE**Ⓔ**N**	J**OO**-B**OW** D**EE**Ⓔ**N**
### Bookstore	### News stand
Shū diàn 书店	Bào tíng 报亭
SH**OO** D**EE**Ⓔ**N**	B**OW** T**EE**NG

Camera shop

Zhào xiàng qì cái shāng diàn   照相器材商店

J**OW** SH**EE**Ⓐ**NG**

CH**EE** TS**Ⓘ**

SH**ⓐ**NG D**EE**Ⓔ**N**

Pharmacy

Yào diàn   药店

Y**OW** D**EE**Ⓔ**N**

SHOPPING LIST

On the following pages you will find some common items you may need to purchase on your trip.

Aspirin

A sī pī lín 阿斯匹林

ah SEE PEE LEEN

Cigarettes

Xiāng yān 香烟

SHEEahNG YahN

Deodorant

Chú chòujì 除臭剂

CHoo CHO-Joo

Clothes

Yī fú 衣服

EE Foo

Film

Jiāo juǎn 胶卷

JEEow JooahN

Perfume

Xiāng shuǐ　香水

SH**EE**②NG　SH⑩②

Razor blades

Tì dāo　剃刀

T**EE**　D⑩

Shampoo

Xiāng bō　香波

SH**EE**②NG　B⑩

Shaving cream

Tì xū dāo　剃须刀

T**EE**　SH⑩　D⑩

Shirt

Chèn yī　衬衣

CH②N　**EE**

Sunglasses

tài yáng jìng / mò jìng　太阳镜／墨镜

T YNG JNG / M JNG

Suntan oil

fáng shài shuāng　防晒霜

FNG SH SHNG

Toothbrushes

yá shuā　牙刷

Y SH

Toothpaste

yá gāo　牙膏

Y G

Water (bottled)

chún jìng shuǐ　纯净水

CHN JNG SH

Water (mineral)

kuàng quán shuǐ　矿泉水

KNG CHN SH

ESSENTIAL SERVICES

THE BANK

As a traveler in a foreign country your primary contact with banks will be to exchange money.

- The unit of currency in China is the **Renembi (RMB).** Take time to familiarize yourself with different bank notes and their respective values.

- It is a good idea to carry traveler's checks rather than cash. Don't display money in public.

- Have your passport handy when changing money. Cash or traveler's checks can be exchanged for Chinese currency at banks and licensed exchange facilities of the Bank of China.

- Money exchanges are also available at major airports and hotels.

- ATMs are readily available in major cities.

- Most major credit cards are accepted; however, it is a good idea to check with your bank to see if your credit card is accepted.

KEY WORDS

Bank

Yín háng   银行

YEEN HAHNG

Exchange office

Huàn waìbì   换外币

HOOAHN WOI-BEE

Money

Qián   钱

CHEEAHN

Money order

Huì piào   汇票

HOOAI PEEOW

Traveler's check

Lǚ xíng zhī piào   旅行支票

LEW SHEENG JUr PEEOW

USEFUL PHRASES

Where is the bank?

Yín háng zài nǎ?   银行在哪？

Y**ⓔ**N H**ⓐ**NG DS**◯** N**ⓐ**h

What time does the bank open?

Yín háng jǐ diǎn kāi mén?   银行几点开门？

Y**ⓔ**N H**ⓐ**NG J**ⓔ**
D**ⓔⓔ**N K**①**-M**ⓐ**N

Where is the exchange office?

Zài nǎ huàn waì bì?   在哪换外币？

DS**◯** N**ⓐ**h H**ⓞⓞⓐ**N W**◯** B**ⓔ**

What time does the exchange office open?

Huàn waì bì de dìfāng jǐ diǎn kāi mén?
换外币的地方几点开门？

H**ⓞⓞⓐ**N W**◯** B**ⓔ** D**ⓤ**h D**ⓔ**-F**ⓐ**NG
J**ⓔ** D**ⓔⓔⓔ**N K**①**-M**ⓤ**N

Can I change dollars here?

Wǒ kě yǐ zài zhè huàn měi yuán ma?
我可以在这换美元吗？

W**ⓐ** K**ⓤ** **ⓔⓔ** DS**◯**
H**ⓞⓞⓐ**N M**ⓐ** Y**ⓞⓞⓐ**N M**ⓐ**h

What is the exchange rate?

Huì lǜ shì duō shǎo?   汇率是多少？

HOOA LEW SHUR DOOah SHOW

I would like large bills.

Wǒ xiǎng yào dà miàn é chāo piào.
我想要大面额钞票

WAH SHEEahNG YOW
DAH MEEEN E CHOW PEEEW

I would like small bills.

Wǒ xiǎng yào xiǎo miàn é chāo piào.
我想要小面额钞票

WAH SHEEahNG YOW
SHEEOW MEEEN
E CHOW PEEEW

I need change.

Wǒ xū yào líng qián.   我需要零钱

WAH SHOO YOW
LENG CHEEEN

Do you have an ATM?

Zhè lǐ yǒu tí kuǎn jī ma?   这里有提款机吗？

JUH LEE YO TEE
KOOahN JEE MAH

POST OFFICE

If you are planning on sending letters and postcards, be sure to send them early so that you don't arrive home before they do.

KEY WORDS

Air mail

Háng kōng yóu jiàn   航空邮件

H⊚NG K⊙NG Y⊙ J⊞⊘N

Letter

Xìn   信

SH⊛N

Post office

Yóu jú   邮局

Y⊙ J⊚

Postcard

Míng xìn piàn   明信片

M⊞NG SH⊛N P⊞⊘N

Stamp

Yóu piào   邮票

Y⊙ P⊞⊚W

USEFUL PHRASES

Where is the post office?

Yóu jú zài nǎ?   邮局在哪？

YO JOO DSI Nah

What time does the post office open?

Yòu jú jǐ diǎn kāi mén?   邮局几点开门？

YO JOO JEE
DEEN KI-MUN

I need…

Wǒ xū yào...   我需要

WO SHOO YOW

I need stamps.

Wǒ xū yào yóu piào.   我需要 邮票

WO SHOO YOW YO PEEOW

I need an envelope.

Wǒ xū yào xìn fēng.   我需要 信封

WO SHOO YOW SHEEN FuhNG

I need a pen.

Wǒ xū yào bǐ.   我需要 笔

WO SHOO YOW BEE

TELEPHONE

Placing phone calls in China can be
a test of will and stamina! Besides
the obvious language barriers, service
can vary greatly from one town to the
next.

- Direct long-distance dials (DDD) and
  international calls (IDD) can be made
  from hotel rooms or roadside telephone
  kiosks.

- International calls can also be made from
  main communications offices.

- Public phones are available in many shops,
  restaurants, and on the street.

- In some large cities, you can buy IP phone
  cards which can save you money.

- Internet services are found in cyber cafes
  and in major hotels.

KEY WORDS

Information

Chá hào tái   查号台

CH⓪ H⓪ T①

Long distance

Cháng tú   长途

CH⓪NG T⓪

Operator

Jiē xiàn yuán   接线员

J⓪⓪ SH⓪⓪N Y⓪⓪N

Phone book

Diàn huà běn   电话本

D⓪⓪N H⓪⓪ B⓪N

Public telephone

Gōng yòng diàn huà   公用电话

G⓪NG Y⓪NG D⓪⓪N H⓪⓪

USEFUL PHRASES

Where is the telephone?

Diàn huà zài nǎ li?   电话在哪里

D㋐㋐Ⓐ N H㏄Ⓐⱨ DSⓄ Nⓐ Lㄸ

Where is the public telephone?

Gōng yōng diàn huà zài nǎ li?   公用电话在哪里?

GⓄNG YⓄNG D㋐㋐Ⓐ N H㏄Ⓐⱨ
DSⓄ Nⓐ Lㄸ

May I use your telephone?

Wǒ kě yǐ yòng yí xià nǐ de diàn huà ma?
我可以用一下你的电话吗?

Wⓐ K㏇ ㄸ
YⓄNG ㄸ SH㋐㋐Ⓐⱨ
Nㄸ DⓊⱨ
D㋐㋐Ⓐ N H㏄Ⓐⱨ Mⓐⱨ

Operator, I don't speak Chinese.

Jiē xiàn yuán, wǒ bú huì jiǎng hàn yǔ.

接线员，我不会讲汉语

JㄸⒺ SH㋐㋐Ⓐ N Y㏄ⓐN
Wⓐⱨ B㏄ H㏄Ⓐ
JㄸⒺNG HⓐN-Y㏄

I want to call this number...

Wǒ xiǎng dǎ zhè gè hào...   我想打这个号

W**ah** SH**EE**a**h**NG D**ah**
J**uh** G**uh** H**ow**...

1 yī 一 **EE**	**2** èr 二 **ah**R	**3** sān 三 S**ah**N
4 sì 四 S**ur**	**5** wǔ 五 W**oo**	**6** liù 六 L**EE**O
7 qī 七 CH**EE**	**8** bā 八 B**ah**	**9** jiǔ 九 J**EE**O
✳	**0** líng L**o**NG	#

SIGHTSEEING AND ENTERTAINMENT

Beijing is the capital and the most modern of cities in the Republic of China. It is home to several ancient palaces, temples, and historical and cultural sites.

CITIES IN CHINA

Beijing　北京
Popular sites in China include the Great Wall, Tian'anmen Square, one of the largest squares in the world built in 1417, and The Forbidden City now known as The Palace Museum.

Shanghai　上海
Shanghai boasts western influence with twenty-story-high buildings reaching skyward and showered with many hotel complexes and villas.

Hong Kong　香港
Hong Kong's natural beauty, rich culture, and accessibility make this city a great gateway to your China travels. Enjoy a beautiful view of the city while riding the Star Ferry through Victoria Harbor.

Xi'an　西安
The city where Chinese culture began its roots and where you can visit the fantastic Qin Terracotta Warrior Museum.

KEY WORDS

Admission

Rùchǎng   入场

ROO   CH@NG

Map

Dì tú   地图

D@E   T@O

Reservation

Yù dìng   预定

Y@O   D@ENG

Ticket

Piào   票

P@EE@W

Tour

Lǔ xíng   旅行 (or) Lǔ yóu   旅游

L@ew   SH@NG / L@ew   Y@O

Tour guide

Lǔ yóu zhǐ nán   旅游指南

L@ew   Y@O   J@Ur   N@N

USEFUL PHRASES

Where is the tourist agency?

Lǚ xíng shè zài nǎ?   旅行社在哪？

L⒠ SH⒠NG SH⒲ DS⒤ N⒜

Where do I buy a ticket?

Wǒ zài nǎ mǎi mén piào?   我在哪买门票？

W⒜ DS⒤ N⒜ M⒤ M⒨N P⒠⒲

How much?

Duō shǎo qián?   多少钱？

D⒪⒜ SH⒪ CH⒠⒩N

How long?

Duō cháng shíhòu jiān?   多长时间？

D⒪⒜ CH⒜NG SH⒲-H⒪ J⒠⒠N

When?

Shénme shíhòu?   什么时候？

SH⒨N-M⒰ SH⒲-H⒪

Where?

Nǎ li?   哪里？

N⒜ L⒠

Do I need reservations?

Wǒ xū yào yù yuē ma?   我需要预约吗？

Wah SHoo Yow
Yoo Yooē Mah

Does the guide speak English?

Zhè gè dǎo yóu jiǎng yīng yǔ ma?
这个导游讲英语吗？

Juh Gou Dow
Yo JEEēNG
YEENG Yoo Mah

How much do children pay?

Xiǎo hái fù duō shǎo qián?   小孩付多少钱？

SHEEow Ho Foo
Dooah SHow CHEEēN

I need your help.

Wǒ xū yào nǐ bāng máng.   我需要你帮忙

Wah SHoo Yow NEE BahNG MoNG

Thank you.

Xiè xie nì.   谢谢你

SHEEē SHEEē NEE

PHRASEMAKER

I'm looking for…

Wǒ zài nǎ néng zhǎo dào…   我在哪能找到

W⒜ DS⦶ N⒜

N⒰NG J⒪ D⒪…

▸ **the Summer Palace**

yí hé yuán   颐和园

⒠ H⒰ Y⒪⒜N

The Summer Palace is a popular local spot featuring
mythical paintings, gardens and Kunming Lake.

▸ **a Tea House**

lǎo shě chá guǎn   老舍茶馆

L⒪ SH⒰ CH⒜ G⒪⒜N

Tea houses offer famous Beijing Opera performances
and Chinese acrobats — a wonderful entertainment
experience. They serve tea, snacks, and food.

▸ **the Great Wall**

cháng chéng   长城

CH⒜NG CH⒰NG

▸ **a swimming pool**

yóu yǒng chí 游泳池

YŌ YŌNG CHŪ

▸ **a movie theater**

diàn yǐng yuàn 电影院

DEEÉN YEENG YOOÁN

▸ **a health club**

jiàn shēn jù lè bù 健身俱乐部

JEEÉN SHUHN JOO LUH BOO

▸ **a tennis court**

wǎng qiú chǎng 网球场

WAhNG CHEEOO CHAhNG

▸ **a golf course**

gāo ěr fū qiú chǎng 高尔夫球场

GOW AhR FOO CHEEOO CHAhNG

HEALTH

Hopefully you will not need medical attention on your trip. If you do, it is important to communicate basic information regarding your condition.

- Check with your insurance company before leaving home to find out if you are covered in a foreign country. You may want to purchase traveler's insurance before leaving home.

- If you take prescription medicine, carry your prescription with you. Have your prescriptions translated into simplified Chinese writing before you leave home.

- Take a small first-aid kit with you. You may want to include basic cold and anti-diarrhea medications. However, you should be able to find most items like aspirin locally.

- In most cases foreigners in large cities like Beijing are sent to the best hospitals and treated by the best doctors in China.

- Hospitals are open seven days a week and sometimes require fees be paid in advance.

KEY WORDS

Ambulance

Jiù hù chē   救护车

J(EE)(oo) H(oo) CH(uh)

Dentist

Yá yī   牙医

Y(ah)   (EE)

Doctor

Yī shēng   医生

(EE) SH(uh)NG

Emergency

Jí zhěn   急诊

J(EE) J(uh)N

Hospital

Yī yuàn   医院

(EE) Y(oo)(ah)N

Prescription

Chǔ fāng   处方

CH(oo) F(ah)NG

USEFUL PHRASES

I am sick.

Wǒ bìng le.   我病了

W(ah) B(E)NG L(uh)

I need a doctor.

Wǒ yào kàn yī shēng.   我要看医生

W(ah) Y(ow) K(ah)N (EE) SH(uh)NG

It's an emergency!

Zhè shì jí zhěn!   这是急诊！

J(uh) SH(r) J(EE) J(un)N

Where is the nearest hospital?

Zuì jìn de yī yuàn zài nǎ li?   最近的医院在哪里？

DS(oo)(A) J(EE)N D(uh)
(EE) Y(oo)(ah)N DS(I) N(ah) L(EE)

Call an ambulance!

Qǐng jiào jiù hù chē!   请叫救护车！

CH(EE)NG J(EE)(ow) H(oo) CH(uh)

I'm allergic to…

Wǒ duì…guò mǐn.　我对。。。过敏

Wah Doo④…Goo⑥h Meen

I'm pregnant.

Wǒ huái yùn le.　我怀孕了

Wah Hoo① Yoon Luh

I'm diabetic.

Wǒ yǒu táng niào bìng.　我有糖尿病

Wah Yo Tahng Neeow Beeng

I have a heart condition.

Wǒ xīnzàng bù hǎo.　我心脏不好

Wah Sheen-Dsahng Boo How

I have high blood pressure.

Wǒ yǒu gāo xuě yā.　我有高血压

Wah Yo Gow Shooĕ Yah

I have low blood pressure.

Wǒ yǒu dī xuě yā.　我有低血压

Wah Yo Dee Shooĕ Yah

PHRASEMAKER

I need...

Wǒ yào...   我要

W_{ah} Y_{ow}...

▶ **a doctor**

kàn yī shēng   看医生

K_{ah}N EE SH_{uh}NG

▶ **a dentist**

kàn yá yī   看牙医

K_{ah}N Y_{ah} EE

▶ **a nurse**

yí gè hù shì   一个护士

EE G_{uh} H_{oo} SH_{ur}

▶ **an optician**

yàn guāng shī   验光师

Y_{ah}N G_{oo}_{ah}NG SH_{ur}

▶ **a pharmacist**

yàojì shī   药剂师

Y_{ow}-J_{EE} SH_{ur}

PHRASEMAKER
(AT THE PHARMACY)

Do you have…

Nǐ yǒu...   你有

N⒠ Y◉…

▶ **aspirin?**

ā sī pī lín ma?   阿斯匹林吗?

⒜ S⒠ P⒠ L⒠N M⒜

▶ **Band-Aids?**

chuàng kě tiē ma?   创可贴 吗?

CH⒪⒜NG K⒪ T⒠⒠ M⒜

▶ **cough syrup?**

zhǐké táng jiāng ma?   止咳糖浆 吗?

J⒰-K⒲ T⒜NG J⒠⒜NG M⒜

▶ **ear drops?**

dī ěr yè ma?   滴耳液 吗?

D⒠ ⒜R̲ Y⒲ M⒜

▶ **eye drops?**

yǎn yào shuǐ ma?   眼药水 吗?

Y⒜N Y⒲ SH⒪⒜ M⒜

BUSINESS TRAVEL

It is important to show appreciation and interest in another person's language and culture, particularly when doing business. A few well-pronounced phrases can make a great impression.

- Exchanging business cards is very important, so be sure to bring a good supply with you.

- It is a good idea to have your business card printed in simplified Chinese and engraved in gold (which implies status).

- Present your business card with the Chinese side facing up, holding it in both hands followed by a handshake. It is a good idea to wait for the recipient to offer the handshake first. He or she may defer to a nod.

- When you receive a card, be sure to examine it and then place it in your card case.

- Business dress is conservative for both men and women and bright-colored clothing is considered inappropriate.

- Gift giving is not a part of Chinese business culture and in most cases will be declined.

- It is not a good idea to wave about or use your hands while speaking.

KEY WORDS

Appointment

Yù yuē   预约

Y(ew)   Y(oo)(e)

Business card

Míng piàn   名片

M(ee)NG   P(ee)(e)N

Meeting

Huì yì   会议

H(oo)(A)   (ee)

Marketing

Shì chǎng   市场

SH(ee)   CH(an)NG

Office

Bàn gōng shì   办公室

B(an)N   G(O)NG   SH(ur)

Presentation

Huì bào   汇报

H(oo)(A)   B(ow)

Telephone

Diàn huà   电话

D(ee)(e)N   H(oo)(ah)

USEFUL PHRASES

I have an appointment.

Wǒ yǒu yù yuē.   我有预约

W**ⓐ** Y**Ⓞ** Y**ⓞⓞ** Y**ⓞⓞⓔ**

My name is…(your name). Pleased to meet you.

Wǒ jiào (…) hěn gāo xìng rèn shi nǐ.

我叫 (…) 很高兴认识你

W**ⓐ** J**ⒺⒺⓐw**… (your name)

H**ⓤⓗ**N G**ⓐw** SH**ⓔ**NG B̲**ⓤⓗ**N SH**Ⓤⓡ** N**ⒺⒺ**

Here is my card.

Zhè shì wǒ de míng piàn.   这是我的名片

J**ⓤⓗ** SH**Ⓤⓡ**

W**ⓐ** D**ⓤⓗ** M**ⒺⒺ**NG P**ⒺⒺⓐ**N

Exchanging business cards should be done with care, holding
your card with both hands with Chinese printing facing the
recipient. It is normal to follow with a handshake.

Can we get an interpreter?

Kě yǐ zhǎo dào yí gè fān yì ma?

可以找到一个翻译吗?

K**ⓞⓤ** **ⒺⒺ** J**ⓐw** D**ⓐw** **ⒺⒺ** G**ⓞⓤ**

F**ⓐⓗ**N **ⒺⒺ** M**ⓐⓗ**

Can you write your address for me?

Nǐ kě yǐ xiě xià nǐ de dì zhǐ ma?

你可以写下你的地址吗？

NEE KOU EE
SHEEe SHEEah NEE Duh
DEE JUr Mah

Can you write your phone number?

Nǐ kě yǐ xiě xià nǐ de diàn huà ma?

你可以写下你的电话吗？

NEE KOU EE
SHEEe SHEEah NEE Duh
DEEeN HOOah Mah

This is my phone number.

Zhè shì wǒ de diàn huà.   这是我的电话

Juh SHuh Wah Duh
DEEeN HOOah

His/Her name is...

Tā jiào...   他／她叫...

Tah JEEow...

Good-bye.

Zaì jiàn.   再见

DSy JEEeN

PHRASEMAKER

I need...

Wǒ xū yào...   我需要

W**ah**   SH**oo**   Y**ow**...

▶ **a computer**

diàn nǎo   电脑

D**EE**ə**N**   N**ow**

▶ **a copy machine**

fù yìn jī   复印机

F**oo**   Y**ee**N   J**ee**

▶ **a conference room**

huì yì shì   会议室

H**oo**A̱   **EE**   SH**uu**

▶ **a fax or fax machine**

chuán zhēn / chuán zhēn jí   传真 / 传真机

CH**ooah**N   J**uh**N / CH**ooah**N   J**uh**N   J**ur**

▶ **an interpreter**

fān yì   翻译

F**ah**N   **EE**

▶ **a lawyer**

lǜ shī   律师

L🕓 SH⑪

▶ **a notary**

gōng zhèng yuán   公证员

G◎NG J⑩NG Y⑩⑳N

▶ **a pen**

bǐ   笔

B㊋

▶ **stamps**

yóu piào   邮票

Y◎ P㊋🕓

▶ **stationery**

bàn gōng yòng pǐn   办公用品

B㊍N G◎NG Y◎NG P㊋N

▶ **typing paper**

dǎ zì zhǐ   打字纸

D㊍ DS⑪ J⑪

GENERAL INFORMATION

China's climate can be compared to that of the United States in that there are four seasons, a primarily temperate climate, and conditions that vary widely from region to region.

SEASONS

Spring

Chūn tiān 春天

CH⓪⓪N T⒠⒠ⓔN

Summer

Xià tiān 夏天

SH⒠⒠⑳ T⒠⒠ⓔN

Autumn

Qiū tiān 秋天

CH⒠⒠⓪⓪ T⒠⒠ⓔN

Winter

Dōng tiān 冬天

D⓪NG T⒠⒠ⓔN

THE DAYS

Monday

Xīng qī yī   星期一

SHEENG CHEE EE

Tuesday

Xīng qī èr   星期二

SHEENG CHEE ahR

Wednesday

Xīng qī sān   星期三

SHEENG CHEE SahN

Thursday

Xīng qī sì   星期四

SHEENG CHEE-Sur

Friday

Xīng qī wǔ   星期五

SHEENG CHEE Woo

Saturday

xīng qī liù   星期六

SHEENG CHEE LEEoo

Sunday

Xīng qī tiān / rì   星期天 / 日

SHEENG CHEE TEEeN / REE

THE MONTHS

January

Yī yuè   一月

Ⓔ Ⓔ Ｙ⓪⓪ⓔ

February

Èr yuè   二月

ⓐ̲Ｒ̲ Ｙ⓪⓪ⓔ

March

Sān yuè   三月

Ｓⓐ̲ｈＮ Ｙ⓪⓪ⓔ

April

Sì yuè   四月

Ｓⓤ̲ｒ Ｙ⓪⓪ⓔ

May

Wǔ yuè   五月

Ｗ⓪⓪ Ｙ⓪⓪ⓔ

June

Liù yuè   六月

Ｌ Ⓔ Ⓔ ⓞ⓪ Ｙ⓪⓪ⓔ

July

Qī yuè   七月

ＣＨ Ⓔ Ⓔ Ｙ⓪⓪ⓔ

August

Bā yuè   八月

Ｂⓐ̲ｈ Ｙ⓪⓪ⓔ

September

Jiǔ yuè   九月

Ｊ Ⓔ Ⓔ ⓞ⓪ Ｙ⓪⓪ⓔ

October

Shí yuè   十月

ＳＨ Ⓔ Ⓔ Ｙ⓪⓪ⓔ

November

Shí yī yuè   十一月

ＳＨ⓪⓪ Ⓔ Ⓔ Ｙ⓪⓪ⓔ

December

Shí èr yuè   十二月

ＳＨ⓪⓪ ⓐ̲Ｒ̲ Ｙ⓪⓪ⓔ

COLORS

Black

Hēi sè   黑色

H(A) S(uh)

White

Bái sè   白色

B(I) S(uh)

Blue

Lán sè   蓝色

L(ah)N S(uh)

Brown

Zōng sè   棕色

DS(O)NG S(uh)

Gray

Hūi sè   灰色

H(oo)(A) S(uh)

Gold

Jīn sè   金色

J(EE)N S(uh)

Orange

Chéng sè   橙色

CH(O)NG S(uh)

Yellow

Huáng sè   黄色

H(oo)(ah)NG S(uh)

Red

Hóng sè   红色

H(O)NG S(uh)

Green

Lǜ sè   绿色

L(ew) S(uh)

Pink

Fěn hóng sè   粉红色

F(uh)N H(O)NG S(uh)

Purple

Zǐ sè   紫色

DS(ur) S(uh)

NUMBERS

0	**1**	**2**
líng 零	yī 一	èr 二
L(E)NG	(EE)	(ah)R

3	**4**	**5**
sān 三	sì 四	wǔ 五
S(uh)N	S(U)	W(oo)

6	**7**	**8**
liù 六	qī 七	bā 八
L(EE)(oo)	CH(EE)	B(ah)

9	**10**	**11**
jiǔ 九	shī 十	shí yī 十一
J(EE)(oo)	SH(EE)	SH(U)-(EE)

12	**13**	**14**
shí èr 十二	shí sān 十三	shí sì 十四
SH(EE)(ah)R	SH(EE)-S(ah)N	SH(U)-S(uh)

15	**16**
shí wǔ 十五	shí lù 十六
SH(U)-W(oo)	SH(U)-L(oo)

17	**18**
shí qī 十七	shí bā 十八
SH(U)-CH(EE)	SH(U)-B(ah)

19	**20**
shí jiǔ　十九	èr shí　二十
SHŬ-JĒŏŏ	ŏ̱R-SHŬr
30	**40**
sān shí　三十	sì shí　四十
Sŏ̱N-SHŬ	SŬr-SHŬ
50	**60**
wǔ shí　五十	liù shí　六十
Wŏŏ-SHŬ	LĒŏŏ-SHŬr
70	**80**
qī shí　七十	bā shí　八十
CHĒ-SHŬ	Bŏ̱h-SHŬ
90	**100**
jiǔ shí　九十	yì bāi　一百
JĒŏŏ-SHŬ	Ē̱-BĪ
1,000	**1,000,000**
yì qiān　一千	yì bǎi wàn　一百万
Ē̱-CHĒĕ̱N	Ē̱-BĪ　Wŏ̱N

CHINESE VERBS

Verbs are the action words of any language. In Mandarin Chinese verbs remain the same.

This means that Chinese verbs have no conjugation because there is only one form for each verb. Because of this, word order in the language is important as it helps you to understand the action as it relates to who is doing what to whom.

Since there is no conjugation in Chinese as compared to English, there is only one form to express the past, present and future tense. For example, in the sentences below; e.g., **I eat** and **I am eating** you will notice in both cases the translation is the same 我吃.

I eat.	**I am eating.**
Wǒ chī　我吃	Wǒ chī　我吃
W⒜ CH⒲	W⒜ CH⒲

Additionally, there are no helping words like am or to, nor articles like a, an, or the. It will take a little while to get used to the absence of these helping words; however, the upside is, you don't have to memorize conjugation tables!

EPLS has chosen Chinese verbs with an emphasis on the traveler but if you learn these verbs you will be on your way to a better understanding of the Chinese language and the path to fluency.

NO VERB CONJUGATIONS

The easiest part of learning Chinese is that there are no verb conjugations. **I, you, he, she, it, we**, and **they** all take the same verb form.

The verb **to be** is **shì**. Notice how its form does not change. This holds true for all Chinese verbs!

I am.	**We are.**
Wǒ **shì.** 我是	Wǒmen **shì.** 我们是
Wah SHœ	Wah-Muhn SHœ
You are.	**You are.** (a group)
Nǐ **shì.** 你是	Nǐmen **shì.** 你们是
Nee SHœ	Nee-Muhn SHœ
He / she / it is.	
Tā **shì.** 他 / 她 / 它是	
Tah SHœ	
They are.	
Tāmen **shì.** 他们是 / 她们是 / 它们是	
Tah-Muhn SHœ	

PHRASEMAKER

I want...

Wǒ xiǎng...   我想

W⊛ SH㊉⊛NG...

He wants...

Tā xiǎng...   他想

T⊛ SH㊉⊛NG...

She wants...

Tā xiǎng...   她想

T⊛ SH㊉⊛NG...

We want...

Wǒmen xiǎng...   我们想

W⊛-M⊛N SH㊉⊛NG...

They want...

Tāmen xiǎng...   他们想

T⊛-M⊛N SH㊉⊛NG...

I don't want...

Wǒ bù xiǎng...   我不想

W⊛ B⊛ SH㊉⊛NG...

▶ **to eat**

chī 吃

CH⊕

▶ **to drink**

hē 喝

H⊛

▶ **to talk**

shuō 说

SW㊅⊛

▶ **to buy**

mǎi 买

M⊙

▶ **to leave**

lí kāi 离开

L㊉ K⊙

▶ **to sleep**

shuì jiào 睡觉

SW㊅⊘ J㊉㊅

PHRASEMAKER

I need...

Wǒ xū yào...   我需要

W@h SH⑩ Y@w...

▶ **to eat**

　chī 吃

　CH⑥

He needs...

Tā xū yào...   我想要

T@h SH⑩ Y@w...

▶ **to drink**

　hē   喝

　H⑥h

She needs...

Tā xū yào...   他希望

T@h SH⑩ Y@w...

▶ **to talk**

　shuō   说

　SW⑩@h

We need...

Wǒmen xū yào...   我们需要

W@h-M⑥N SH⑩ Y@w...

▶ **to buy**

　mǎi   买

　M⑥

They need...

Tāmen xū wǎng...   他们需要

T@h-M⑥N SH⑩ Y@w...

▶ **to leave**

　lí kāi 离开

　L⑥ K①

I don't need...

Wǒ bù xū yào...   我不需要

W@h B⑩ SH⑩ Y@w...

▶ **to sleep**

　shuì jiào 睡觉

　SW⑩④ J⑥⑩w

NEGATIVES

A simple way to form a negative in Chinese is to add **bu** (not) in front of the verb.

I eat.	**I don't eat.**
Wǒ chī 我吃	Wǒ **bù** chī 我不吃
W@h CH@	W@h B@ CH@

I want.	**I don't want.**
Wǒ yào 我要	Wǒ **bù** yào 我不要
W@h Y@	W@h B@ Y@

I understand.	**I don't understand.**
Wǒ dǒng 我懂	Wǒ **bù** dǒng 我不懂
W@h D@NG	W@h B@ D@NG

A notable execption to the above pattern is the verb **to have**, which takes the word **méi** before it to say **I don't have.**

I have.	**I don't have.**
Wǒ yǒu. 我有	Wǒ **méi** yǒu. 我没有
W@h Y@	W@h M@ Y@

150 VERBS

Here are some essential verbs that will carry you a long way towards learning Chinese with the EPLS Vowel Symbol System!

to add

tiānjiā 添加

T㋎㋎N-J㋎㋑

to allow

yǔnxǔ 允许

㋎㋒N-CH㋒

to answer

huí dá 回答

H㋵㋎ D㋐

to arrive

dàodá 到达

D㋌ D㋐

to ask

wèn 问

W㋍N

to attack

gōng jī 攻击

G㋵NG CH㋎

to attend

chūxí 出席

CH㋵-SH㋎

to bake

kǎo 烤

K㋌

to be

shì 是

SH㋒

to be able

néng 能

N㋍NG

to beg

qiú 求

CHEEO

to begin

kāishǐ 开始

KI-SHur

to believe

xiāngxìn 相信

SHEEahNG-SHEEN

to bother

má fán 麻烦

Mah FahN

to break

dǎpò 打破

Dah-POO

to breathe

hūxī 呼吸

WHoo-HEE

to bring

dài 带

DI

to build

jiànshè 建设

JEEN-SHuh

to burn

shāoshāng 烧伤

SHow-SHahNG

to buy

mǎi 买

MI

to cancel

qǔ xiāo 取消

CHuu SHow

to call

dǎ diàn huà 打电话

Dah DEEahN WHah

to carry

ná 拿

Nah

to change

gǎibiàn 改变

GI-BEEeN

to chew

jǔjué 咀嚼

J㏿-J㏿

to clean

qīngjié 清洁

CH㏿N-J㏿

to climb

pá 爬

P㏿

to close

guānbì 关闭

G㏿N-B㏿

to come

lái 来

L㏿

to cook

zuò fàn 做饭

Z㏿ F㏿N

to count

shǔ 数

SH㏿

to cry

kū 哭

K㏿

to cut

xuējiǎn 削减

SH㏿-J㏿

to dance

tiàowǔ 跳舞

T㏿-W㏿

to decide

jué dìng 决定

J㏿ D㏿NG

to depart

líkāi 离开

L㏿ K㏿

disturb

dǎ rǎo 打扰

D㏿ R㏿

to do

zuò 做

Z㏿

to drink

hē　喝

H(uh)

to drive

kāichē　开车

K(i)-CH(uh)

to dry

nòng gān　弄干

N(o)NG　G(ah)N

to earn

zhuàn　赚

CH(oo)(ah)N

to eat

chī　吃

CH(ee)

to explain

jiě shì　解释

J(ee)(e)　SH(ee)

to enjoy

xiǎngshòu　享受

SH(ee)(ah)NG-SH(o)

to enter

jìnrù　进入

CH(ee)N-B(oo)

to feel

gǎnjué　感觉

G(ah)N-J(oo)(e)

to fight

dǎ　打

D(ah)

to fill

tiánbǔ　填补

T(ee)(e)N-B(oo)

to find

zhǎo　找

CH(ow)

to finish

wánchéng　完成

W(ah)N-CH(o)NG

to fit

shìhé　适合

SH(ee)-H(o)

to fix

xiūfù 修复

SH(oo)-F(oo)

to fly

fēi 飞

F(a)

to follow

gēnsuí 跟随

G(uh)N-SW(a)

to forgive

yuán liàng 原谅

Y(oo)(a)N L(ee)(a)NG

to get

huòdé 获得

H(oo)(a)-D(uh)

to give

gěi 给

G(a)

to go

qù 去

CH(ee)

to greet

yíngjiē 迎接

Y(o)NG-SH(ee)(e)

to happen

fāshēng 发生

F(ah)-SH(uh)NG

to have

yǒu 有

Y(ow)

to hear

tīng 听

T(ee)NG

to help

bāngzhù 帮助

B(ah)NG-J(oo)

to hide

yǐncáng 隐藏

Y(ee)N-TS(a)NG

to hit

dǎ 打

D(ah)

to imagine

xiǎngxiàng   想象

SH(ah)NG-SH(ah)NG

to improve

gǎi shàn   改善

G(I)   SH(ah)N

to jump

tiào   跳

T(EE)(Ow)

to kiss

wěn   吻

W(ah)N

to know

zhī dào   知道

ZH(EE)   D(Ow)

to laugh

xiào   笑

SH(EE)(Ow)

to learn

xuéxí   学习

SH(EE)(E)-SH(EE)

to leave

líkāi   离开

L(EE)-K(I)

to lie (not the truth)

sāhuǎng   撒谎

S(ah)-WH(ah)NG

to lift

tí shēng   提升

T(EE)   SH(uh)NG

to like

xǐ huān   喜欢

SH(EE)-WH(ah)N

to listen

tīng   听

T(EE)NG

to live

zhù   住

J(oo)

to look

kàn   看

K(ah)N

to lose

shīqù 失去

SHEE-CHEE

to love

ài 爱

I

to make

shǐ 使

SHR

to measure

cè liáng 测量

KU LEEANG

to miss

cuòguò 错过

KO-GWah

to move

yídòng 移动

YEE-DONG

to need

xūyào 需要

SHOO-YOW

to offer

tígōng 提供

TEE-GONG

to open

dǎkāi 打开

Dah-KI

to order

mìnglìng 命令

MONG-LONG

to pack

shōushí 收拾

SHO-SHR

to pass

tōngguò 通过

TONG-GWah

to pay (for)

zhīfù 支付

JEE-FOO

to play

wán 玩

WON

to pretend

jiǎzhuāng   假装

JEE(ah)-JOO(ah)NG

to print

dǎyìn   打印

D(ah)-YEEN

to promise

chéngnuò   承诺

CHONG-NWO(ah)

to pronounce

fāyīn   发音

F(ah)-YEEN

to push

tuī   推

TW(A)

to put

fàng   放

F(ah)NG

to quit

jiè   戒

JEE(e)

to read

dú   读

DOO

to receive

shōu dào   收到

SHO DOW

to recomend

jiànyì   建议

JEE(e)N-YEE

to rent

zū   租

ZOO

remember

jì zhù   记住

SHEE CHOO

to rescue

yíngjiù   营救

YENG-CHEE(o)

to rest

xiūxí   休息

SHEE(o)-SHEE

to return

fǎnhuí 返回

F⒜N-HW⒜

to run

pǎo 跑

P⒲

to say

shuō 说

SH⒪⒪⒜h

to see

kàn 看

K⒜N

to sell

chūshòu 出售

CH⒪⒪-SH⊘

to send

sòng 送

S⊘NG

to show

xiǎnshì 显示

SH⒠⒠ⓔ SH⒰

to sign

qiān shǔ 签署

CH⒠⒠ⓔN-SH⒪⒪

to sing

chàng 唱

CH⒜NG

to sit

zuò 坐

Z⓪⒜

to sleep

shuìjiào 睡觉

SH⒪⒪⒠-J⒠⒠⒲

to smoke

xī yān 吸烟

SH⒠⒠ Y⒠N

to smile

wē xiào 微笑

W⒜ SH⒠⒠⒲

to speak

fāyán 发言

F⒜h-Y⒠N

to spell

pīnxiě   拼写

P(EE)N-SH(EE)(s)

to spend

huā   花

H(00)(ah)

to stand

zhàn   站

J(a)N

to start / begin

kāishǐ   开始

K(I) SH(U)

to stay

liú   留

L(EE)(O)

to stop

tíngzhǐ   停止

T(a)NG-SH(EE)

to study

xué xí   学习

SH(EE)(s) SH(EE)

to succeed

chéng gōng   成功

CH(u)NG-G(O)NG

to swim

yóuyǒng   游泳

Y(O)-Y(O)NG

to take

cǎiqǔ   采取

CH(I)-CH(OO)

to talk

tán   谈

T(a)N

to taste

pǐncháng   品尝

P(EE)N-CH(a)NG

to teach

jiāo   教

J(EE)(OW)

to tell

gàosù   告诉

G(OW)-S(OO)

to touch

chùmō 触摸

CHOO-MWah

to travel

lǚxíng 旅行

Lew-SHENG

to try

chángshì 尝试

CHONG-SHOO

to understand

lǐjiě 理解

LEE-JEEe

to use

shǐyòng 使用

SHEE-YONG

to wait

děng 等

DONG

to warn

jǐng gào 警告

JEENG GOW

to walk

zǒu 走

ZO

to want

xiǎng 想

SHEEaNG

to wash

xǐ 洗

SHEE

to win

yíng 赢

YONG

to work

gōngzuò 工作

GOONG TSWah

to worry

dānxīn 担心

DahN SHEEN

to write

xiě 写

SHEEe

DICTIONARY

Each English entry is followed by the Pīnyīn spelling, Chinese characters, and then the EPLS Vowel Symbol System.

A

a lot   hěn duō   很多   H⒰N D⒪

a, an   yí gè   一个   ⓔ Y⒤-G⒠

able   néng   能   N⒪NG

accident   shì-gù   事故   SH⒥-G⒪

accommodation   zhù sù   住宿 J⒪ S⒪

account   zhàng hù   账户   J⒜NG H⒪

address   dì zhǐ   地址   D⒠-J⒤

admission   rù chǎng   入场   B⒪-CH⒜NG

afraid   hài pà   害怕   H⒤ P⒜

after   yǐ-hòu   以后   ⒠-H⒪

afternoon   xià wǔ   下午   SHⒺ⒜-W⒪

agency   dài lǐ   代理   D⒤-L⒠

air-conditioning   kōngtiáo   空调   K⒪NG-TⒺ⒪

aircraft   fēi jì   飞机   F⒜ J⒤

airline   háng kōng gōng-sī   航空公司   H⒜NG-K⒪NG G⒪NG-S⒤

airport   fēijīchǎng   飞机场   F⒜-JⒺ-CH⒜NG

aisle   guòdào   过道   G⒪⒜-D⒪

all quánbù / dōu 全部／都 CH@@N-B@ / D@

almost jīhū 几乎 J@-H@

alone dāndú 单独 D@N-D@

also yě 也 Y@

always zǒng shì 总是 DS@NG-SH@

ambulance jiù hù chē 救护车 J@@-H@ CH@

American měi guó rén 美国人 M@-G@@-B@N

and hé 和 H@

another lìng yí gè 另一个 L@NG-@-G@

anything rènhé dōngxi 任何东西
   B@N-H@ D@NG-SH@

apartment gōng yù 公寓 G@NG Y@

appetizers kāi wèi cài 开胃菜 K@ W@ TS@

apple píngguǒ 苹果 P@NG-G@@

appointment yù huē 预约 Y@-Y@@

April sì yuè 四月 S@-Y@@

arrival dào dá 到达 D@ D@

ashtray yān huī gāng 烟灰缸 Y@N-H@@ G@NG

aspirin ā sī pī lín 阿斯匹林 @-S@-P@-L@N

attention zhù yì 注意 J@-@

August bā yuè 八月 B@-Y@@

author zuò zhě 作者 DS@@-J@

automobile qì chē 汽车 CH@-CH@

Autumn   qiū tiān   秋天   CH_{OO}-T_{EE}_EN

avenue   dà jiē   大街   D_{ah}-J_{EE}_{uh}

awful   zāo gāo de   糟糕的   TS_{OW} G_{OW} D_{uh}

B

baby   yīng'er   婴儿   Y_{EE}NG-_{ah}R

babysitter   bǎo mǔ   保姆   B_{OW}-M_{OO}

bacon   xūnròu   熏肉   SH_{OO}N-R_O

bad   huài   坏   H_{OO}_I

bag   dài / dàizi   袋 / 袋子   D_I / D_I-DS_{EE}

baggage   xínglǐ   行李   SH_ENG-L_{EE}

baked   kǎo de   烤的   K_{OW} D_{uh}

bakery   gāo diǎn diàn   糕点店   G_{OW}-D_{EE}_EN D_{EE}_EN

banana   xiāng jiāo   香蕉   SH_{EE}_{ah}NG-J_{EE}_{OW}

Band-Aid   chuàng kě tiē   创可贴
    CH_{OO}_{ah}NG K_{OU} T_{EE}_E

bank   yínháng   银行   Y_EN-H_{ah}NG

barbershop   lǐfà diàn   理发店   L_{EE}-F_{ah} D_{EE}_EN

bartender   jiǔ bā zhāo dài   酒吧招待
    J_{EE}_{OO} B_{ah} J_{OW} D_I

bath   yùgāng   浴缸   Y_{OO}-G_{ah}NG

bathing suit   yóuyǒngyī   游泳衣   Y_O-Y_ONG-_{EE}

bathroom (for baths)—yùshì   浴室   Y_{OO}-SH_E

battery   diànchí   电池   D_{EE}_EN-CH_E

beach   hǎitān   海滩   HĪ-TahN

beautiful   měilì piàoliàng   美丽／漂亮   MA-LEE PEEo-LEEoNG

beauty shop   fàláng   发廊   Fah-LONG

bed   chuáng   床   CHooaNG

beef   niúròu   牛肉   NEEo-Ro

beer   píjiǔ   啤酒   PEE-JEEo

bellman   xínglǐ yuán   行李员   SHeNG-Lee ooaN

belt   pídái   皮带   PEE-DĪ

big   dà   大   Dah

bill   zhàng dān   帐单   JoNG DahN

black   hēi sè   黑色   HA So

blanket   tǎnzi   毯子   TahN-ZUr

blue   lán sè   蓝色   LahN So

boat   chuán   船   CHooaN

book   shū   书   SHoo

bookstore   shūdiàn   书店   SHoo-DEEoN

border   biānjiè   边界   BEEeN-JEEe

boy   nánhái   男孩   NahN-HĪ

bracelet   shǒuzhuó   手镯   SHĪ-Jooa

brakes   shā chē   刹车   SHah-CHuh

bread   miànbāo   面包   MEEeN-Bow

breakfast   zǎofàn   早饭   DSow-FahN

broiled   kǎo de   烤的   KOW DUH

brother (older)   gē ge   哥哥   GUH GUH

brother (younger)   dì di   弟弟   DEE GEE

brown   zōngsè   棕色   DSONG-SUH

brush   shuāzi   刷子   SHOOAH-DSUr

building   lóufáng / jiàn zhù wù   楼房 / 建筑物
LO-FONG / JEEEN-JOO WOO

bus   gōng gòng qì chē   公共汽车
GONG GONG CHEE-CHUH

bus station   qìchē zhàn   汽车站   CHEE-CHUH JON

bus stop   qìchē zhàn   汽车站   CHEE-CHUH JON

business   shēngyì   生意   SHUHNG-EE

butter   huángyóu   黄油   HOOONG-YO

buy (I)   wǒ mǎi   我买   WOH-MY

C

cab   chūzū qìchē   出租汽车   CHOO-DSOO CHEE-JUH

call (I)   jiào   叫   JEEOW

call   gěi... dǎdiànhuà   给   打电话
GAY DAH-DEEEN-HOOAH

camera   zhàoxiàngjī   照相机   JOW-SHEEONG-JEE

candy   tángguǒ   糖果   TONG-GOOOH

car   qìchē   汽车   CHEE-CHUH

carrot   hú luóbo   胡萝卜   HOO LOOOAH-BO

castle chéng bǎo 城堡 CHONG-BOW

cathedral dà jiào táng 大教堂 DA JEEOW TONG

celebration qìng zhù 庆祝 CHONG-JOO

center zhōngxīn 中心 JONG-SHEEN

cereal màipiàn 麦片 MY-PEEEN

chair yǐ zi 椅子 EE-DSEE

champagne xiāngbīnjiǔ 香槟酒
SHEEANG-BEEN-JEEOO

change (to) huàn qián 换钱 HOOAN CHEEEN

change (money) língqián 零钱 LONG-CHEEEN

cheap pián yi 便宜 PEEEN-EE

check (restaurant bill) zhàngdān 帐单 JONG-DAHN

cheers! gānbēi 干杯 GAHN-BAY

cheese nǎilào 奶酪 NI-LOW

chicken jī 鸡 EE

child xiǎohái 小孩 SHEEOW-HOW

China zhōngguó 中国 JONG-GWO

Chinese (language) zhōngwén 中文 JONG-GWON

Chinese (person) xiǎohái 中国人
JONG-GWO RON

chocolate qiǎokèlì 巧克力 CHEEOW-KO-LEE

church jiàotáng 教堂 JEEOW-TONG

cigar xuě jiā 雪茄 SHOOE-JEEAH

cigarette xiāngyān 香烟 SHEE-ENG-Y@N

city chéngshì 城市 CH@NG-SH@

clean gānjìng 干净 G@N-J@NG

close (to) kào jìn 靠近 K@ J@N

closed guānmén 关门 G@@@N-M@N

clothes yīfu 衣服 EE-F@

cocktail jīwěijiǔ 鸡尾酒 JEE-W@-J@@

coffee kāfēi 咖啡 K@H-F@

cold (temperture) lěng 冷 L@NG

comb shūzi 梳子 SH@@-DS@

come (I) wǒ lái 我来 W@H L@

company gōngsī 公司 G@NG-S@

computer diànnǎo 电脑 D@@N-N@

concert yīnyuè huì 音乐会 @N-Y@@ H@@

condom bìyùntào 避孕套 B@-Y@N-T@

conference huìyì 会议 H@@@-@

conference room huìyìshì 会议室 H@@@-@-SH@

congratulations gōngxǐ 恭喜 G@NG-SH@

contraceptive bì yùn yào 避孕药 B@ Y@N Y@

copy machine fù yìn jī 复印机 F@ Y@N J@

xerox fùyìn 复印 F@-@N

corn yùmǐ 玉米 Y@-M@

cough syrup zhǐ ké táng jiāng   止咳糖浆

JⓊr KⓄⓌ TⒶNG JEEⒶNG

cover charge fú wù fèi   服务费   FⓄⓄ WⓄⓄ FⒶ

crab páng xiè   螃蟹   PⓄNG SHEEⒺ

cream nǎiyóu   奶油   NⒾ-YⓄ

credit card xìnyòng kǎ   信用卡   SHⒺN-YⓄNG KⒶ

cup bēizi   杯子   BⒶ-ZEE

customs hǎiguān   海关   HⒾ-GⓄⓄⒶⓗN

D

dance (I) tiào wǔ   跳舞   TEEⓌ WⓄⓄ

dangerous wēixiǎn   危险   WⒶ-SHEEⒶN

date (calender) rìqī 日期   BⒺ-CHEE

day tiān   天   TEEⒺN

December shí ' èr yuè   十二月   SHⓌ ⒶB YⓄⓄⒺ

delicious hǎochī   好吃   HⓄⓌ-CHEE

delighted kuài lè   快乐   KⓄⓄ⒵-LⓌ

dentist yáyī   牙医   YⒶ-EE

deodorant chúchòujì   除臭剂   CHⓄⓄ-CHⓄ JⒺ

department bùmén   部门   BⓄⓄ-MⒶN

departure chūfā   出发   CHⓄⓄ-FⒶⓗ

dessert tián diǎn   甜点   TEEⒶN-DEEⒶN

detour wānlù   弯路   WⒶⓗN-LⓄⓄ

diabetic tángniàobìng 糖尿病 T⊙NG N⊛⊛-B⊛NG

diarrhea lā dùzi 拉肚子 L⊛-D⊙-Z⊛

dictionary zì diǎn 字典 Z⊛-D⊛⊛N

dinner wǎncān 晚餐 W⊛N-TS⊛N

dining room cāntīng 餐厅 K⊛N-T⊛NG

direction fāngxiàng 方向 F⊛NG-CH⊛⊛NG

dirty zāng 脏 DS⊛NG

disabled cán jí de 残疾的 TS⊛N-J⊛ D⊛

discount zhékòu 折扣 J⊛-K⊘

distance jù lí 距离 J⊙-L⊛

doctor yīshēng 医生 ⊛-SH⊙NG

document wénjiàn 文件 W⊛N-J⊛⊛N

dollar yuán 元 Y⊙⊛N

down xià 下 SH⊛⊛

downtown shìzhōngxīn 市中心 SH⊛-J⊙NG-CH⊛N

drink (beverage) yǐn liào (n) 饮料 ⊛N-L⊛⊛

drugstore yàodiàn 药店 Y⊛-D⊛⊛N

dry cleaner gān xǐ diàn 干洗店
  G⊛N SH⊛ D⊛⊛N

duck yāzi 鸭子 Y⊛-Z⊛

E

ear ěrduō 耳朵 ⊛B-D⊙⊛

ear drops ěrzhuì 耳坠 ⊛B-J⊙⊘

early zǎo 早 DS⊕

east dōng 东 D⊙NG

easy róngyì 容易 R⊙NG-⊛

eat (I) chī 吃 CH⊕

egg jīdàn 鸡蛋 J⊕-D⊛N

eggs (fried) jiān jīdàn 煎鸡蛋 J⊕⊛N J⊕-D⊛N

eggs (scrambled) chǎo jīdàn 炒鸡蛋 CH⊙w J⊕-D⊛N

electricity diàn 电 D⊕⊛N

elevator diàntī 电梯 D⊕⊛N-T⊕

embassy dàshǐguǎn 大使馆 D⊛-SH⊕-G⊙⊛N

emergency jǐnjí qíngkuàng 紧急情况 J⊛NG-J⊛ CH⊛NG K⊙⊛NG

English yīngyǔ 英语 Y⊛NG-Y⊙

enough! gòu le! 够了 G⊘-L⊎

entrance rù kǒu 入口 R⊛ K⊘

envelope xìnfēng 信封 SH⊛N-F⊎NG

evening wǎnshàng 晚上 W⊛N-SH⊛NG

everything yíqiè 一切 Y⊛-CH⊕⊛

excellent fēicháng hǎo 非常好 F⊛-CH⊛NG H⊙w

excuse me láojià 劳驾 L⊙-J⊕⊛

exit chūkǒu 出口 CH⊙⊙-K⊘

expensive guì 贵 G⊙⊛⊘

eye yǎnjīng 眼睛 Y@N-J@NG

eye drops yǎnyàoshuǐ 眼药水 Y@N-Y@-SH@@

F

face liǎn 脸 L@@N

far yuǎn 远 Y@@N

fare chē fèi 车费 CH@ F@

fast kuài 快 K@@

father fù qīn 父亲 F@ CH@N

fax, fax machine chuánzhēn jī 传真机
　　CH@@N-J@N J@

February èryuè 二月 @B-Y@@

few shǎo 少 SH@

film (movie) diànyǐng 电影 D@@N-Y@NG

film jiāojuǎn 胶卷 J@@-J@@N

finger shǒuzhǐ 手指 SH@-J@

fire extinguisher miè huǒ qì 灭火器
　　M@@ H@@ CH@

fire huǒ 火 H@@

fire! zháo huǒ le! 着火了 J@ H@@ L@

first dìyī 第一 D@-@

fish yú 鱼 Y@

flight hángbān 航班 H@NG-B@N

florist shop huā diàn 花店 H@@ D@@N

flower huā 花 H00ah

food shíwù 食物 SH0-W00

foot jiǎo 脚 JEEOW

fork chāzi 叉子 CHah-ZEE

french fries zhá shǔ tiáo 炸薯条 Jah SH00 TEEOW

fresh xīnxiān 新鲜 SHEEN-SHEEEN

Friday xīngqī wǔ 星期五 SHEENG-CHEE W00

fried jiān 煎 JEEEN

friend péngyǒu 朋友 P0NG-Y0

fruit shuǐguǒ 水果 SH00A-G00ah

funny kě xiào 可笑 K0U SHEEOW

G

gas station jiāyóu zhàn 加油站 GEEah-Y0 JahN

gasoline qìyóu 汽油 CHEE-Y0

gate mén 门 M0N

gentleman shēng shì 绅士 SH0NG SH0

gift lǐwù 礼物 LEE-W0

girl lǚ hái 女孩 L0W-H0

glass (drinking) bō li bēi 玻璃杯 B0-LEE BA

glasses (eye) yǎnjìng 眼镜 YahN-J0NG

glove shǒu tào 手套 SH0-T0W

go qù 去 CH0

gold   jīn   金   J⒠N

golf   gāo ěrfū   高尔夫   G⒪ⓦ   ⓐⒽ-F⒬

golf course   gāo' ěrfū qiú chǎng   高尔夫球场

    G⒪ⓦ   ⓐⒽ-F⒬   CH⒠⒬   CH⒜NG

good   hǎo   好   H⒪ⓦ

good-bye   zàijiàn   再见   DS⦰-J⒠⒜N

goose   é   鹅   ⓤ

grape   pú táo   葡萄   P⒬-T⒪ⓦ

grateful   gǎn jī de   感激的   G⒜N   J⒠   D⒰Ⓗ

gray   huīsè   灰色   H⒬Ⓐ-S⒰ⓦ

green   lǜ sè   绿色   L⒰ⓦ   S⒰ⓦ

grocery store   zá huò diàn   杂货店

    DS⒜-H⒬⒪   D⒠⒜N

group   tuántǐ   团体   T⒬⒜N-T⒠

guide   dǎoyóu   导游   D⒪ⓦ-Y⦰

H

hair   tóufa   头发   T⦰-F⒜Ⓗ

hairbrush   fàshuā   发刷   F⒜-SH⒬ⓐ

haircut   lǐfà   理发   L⒠   F⒜

ham   huǒtuǐ   火腿   H⒬ⓐ-T⒬ⓔ

hamburger   hànbǎo bāo   汉堡包   H⒜N-B⒪   B⒪ⓦ

hand   shǒu   手   SH⦰

happy   gāoxìng   高兴   G⒪ⓦ-SH⒜NG

have (I) yǒu 有 YO

he tā 他 Tah

head tóu 头 TO

headache tóuténg 头疼 TO-TONG

health club jiànshēn fáng 健身房 JEEN-SHUHN FONG

heart condition xīn zàng bìng 心脏病 SHEEN DSONG BONG

heart xīnzàng 心脏 SHEEN JEEONG

heat nuǎnqì 暖气 NOOAHN-CHEE

hello nǐ hǎo 你好 NEE HOW

help! (emergency) jiù mìng 救命 JEEO-MONG

here zhè' er 这儿 JOOAHR

holiday jiàqī 假期 JEEAH-CHEE

hospital yīyuàn 医院 EE-YOOAN

hot dog rè gǒu 热狗 RO GO

hotel lǚ guǎn 旅馆 LOO-GOOAN

hour xiǎoshí 小时 SHEEow-SHO

how zěn me 怎么 DSON-MUH

hurry up! gǎnkuài 赶快 GAHN-KOOEYE

husband zhāng fū 丈夫 JONG FOO

I

I wǒ 我 WO

ice bīng 冰 B⬡NG

ice cream bīng ji líng 冰激凌 B⬡NG J⬡-L⬡NG

ice cubes bīng kuài 冰块 B⬡NG K⬡⬡

ill bìng le 病了 B⬡NG-L⬡

important zhòngyào 重要 ZH⬡NG-Y⬡

indigestion xiāohuà bù liáng 消化不良
SH⬡⬡ H⬡⬡ B⬡ L⬡⬡NG

information xìnxī 信息 SH⬡N-SH⬡

inn xiǎo lǚ guǎn 小旅馆 SH⬡⬡ L⬡ G⬡⬡N

interpreter fānyì 翻译 F⬡N-⬡

J

jacket jiákè 夹克 J⬡-K⬡

jam guǒjiàng 果酱 G⬡⬡-J⬡⬡NG

January yīyuè 一月 ⬡-Y⬡⬡

jewelry zhūbǎo 首饰 J⬡-B⬡

jewelry store zhūbǎo diàn 首饰店 J⬡-B⬡ D⬡⬡N

job gōngzuò 工作 G⬡NG-DS⬡⬡

juice guǒzhī 果汁 G⬡⬡-ZH⬡

July qīyuè 七月 CH⬡-Y⬡⬡

June liùyuè 六月 L⬡⬡-Y⬡⬡

K

ketchup fānqié jiàng 番茄酱
F⬡NG-CH⬡ J⬡NG

key yàoshi 钥匙 YOW-SHUr

kiss (literally: "May I kiss you.") qīn 亲 CHEEN

knife dāozi 刀子 DOW-ZUr

know (I) zhīdào 知道 JEE-DOW

L

ladies' restroom nǚ xǐ shǒu jiān 女洗手间
NEW SHEE SHO JEEEN

lady nǚ shì 女士 NEW-SHUr

lamb yángròu 羊肉 YANG-ROW

language yǔyán 语言 YOO-YAN

large dà 大 DAH

late wǎn 晚了 WAHN

laundry xǐyī diàn 洗衣店 SHEE-EE DEEEN

lawyer lǜ shī 律师 LEW-SHUr

left (direction) zuǒbiān 左边 DSOOah-BEEEN

leg tuǐ 腿 TOOay

lemon níngméng 柠檬 NENG-MONG

less shǎo 少 SHOW

letter xìn 信 SHEEN

lettuce shēng cài 生菜 SHUHNG TSO

light dēng 灯 DUHNG

like (I) xǐhuān 喜欢 SHEE-HOOahN

lip chún 唇 CHOON

lipstick kǒuhóng 口红 KO-HONG

little (amount) shǎo 少 SHOW

little (size) xiǎo 小 SHEEOW

live (to) huó 活 HOOO

lobster lóngxiā 龙虾 LONG-SHEEah

long cháng 长 CHONG

lost mí lùle (adj) 迷路了 MEE LOO-Lun

love ài 爱 I

luck yùnqi 运气 YON-CHEE

luggage xínglǐ 行李 SHEENG-LEE

lunch wǔfàn 午饭 WOO-FON

M

maid fù wù yuán 服务员 FOO WOO YOOON

mail yóujiàn 邮件 YO-JEEON

makeup huàzhuāng 化妆 HOOah-JOOahNG

man nánrén 男人 NON-BON

manager jīnglǐ 经理 JENG LEE

map dìtú 地图 DEE-TOO

March sānyuè 三月 SahN-YOOE

market shìchǎng 市场 SHOO-CHONG

match (light) huǒchái 火柴 HOOah-CHI

May wǔyuè 五月 WOO-YOOE

mayonnaise dànhuáng jiàng 蛋黄酱
DAN-HOONG JEEONG

meal fàn 饭 FAN

meat ròu 肉 RO

mechanic jìgōng 技工 JEE-GONG

meeting huì yì 会议 HOOA EE

mens' restroom nán cèsuǒ 男厕所
NAN SA-SOOan

menu càidān 菜单 TSO-DaN

message liú yán 留言 LEEoo-YaN

milk niúnǎi 牛奶 NEEoo-NI

mineral water kuàngquán shuǐ 矿泉水
KOOANG-CHOOaN SHOOa

minute fēnzhōng 分钟 FuN-JONG

Miss xiǎojiě 小姐 SHEEow-JEEa

mistake cuòwù 错误 TSOo-Wo

misunderstanding wùhuì 误会 Wo-HOOA

moment piàn kè 片刻 PEEAN Ko

Monday xīng qī yī 星期一 CHEENG-CHEE EE

money qián 钱 CHEEAN

month yuè 月 Yoo

monument jìniànbēi 纪念碑 JEE-NEEAN-BA

more gèng duō 更多 GaNG Dooa

morning zǎochén 早晨 DSow-CHaN

mosque qīng zhēn si 清真寺 CH㊉NG-J㊲N S㊂

mother mǔqīn 母亲 M㊍-CH㊉N

mountain shān 山 SH㋐N

movies diànyǐng 电影 D㊎㊁N-Y㋐NG

Mr. xiānsheng 先生 SH㊎㊁N-SH㊲NG

Mrs. fūrén 夫人 F㊍-B㋐N

much (too) duō 多 D㊍㋐

museum bówùguǎn 博物馆 B㋔-W㊍-G㊍㋐N

mushrooms mógu 蘑菇 M㋔-G㊍

music yīnyuè 音乐 ㋐N-Y㊍㊁

mustard jièmo 芥末 J㊎㊁-M㋔

N

nail polish zhī jia yóu 指甲油 J㊎-J㊎㋐ Y㋔

name míngzi 名字 M㋐NG-DS㊎

napkin cān jīn zhǐ 餐巾纸 TS㋐N-J㊎N ZH㊂

napkins (sanitary) wèi shēng jīn 卫生巾 W㋐-SH㊲NG J㊎N

near jìn 近 J㋐N

neck bózi 脖子 B㋔-Z㊎

need (I) wǒ xūyào 我需要 W㋐ SH㊍-Y㋔

never yǒngbù 永不 Y㋔NG-B㊍

newspaper bàozhǐ 报纸 B㋔-J㊂

news stand bàotān 报摊 B㋔-T㋐N

next time   xià cì   下次   SHEE-TSEE

night   yèwǎn   夜晚   YAH-WAN

nightclub   yè zǒnghuì   夜总会   YAH DSONG-HOOAY

no   bú shì   不是   BOO SHAH

no smoking   qǐng wù xī yān   请勿吸烟
CHEENG WOO SHEE YAHN

noon   zhōng wǔ   中午   ZHONG WOO

north   běi   北   BAY

notary   gōng zhèng rén   公证人   GONG JAHN RAN

November   shíyīyuè   十一月   SHOO-EE-YOOEH

now   xiànzài   现在   SHEEAN-DSIGH

number   hàomǎ   号码   HOW-MAH

nurse   hùshi   护士   HOO-SHUU

O

occupied   bèi zhàn yòng de   被占用的
BAY DSAN YONG DUH

ocean   hǎiyáng   海洋   HIGH-YANG

October   shíyuè   十月   SHOO-YOOEH

officer   guān yuán   官员   GOOAHN-YOOAHN

oil   yóu   油   YO

omelet   dànjiǎo   蛋饺   DAN-JEEAH

one-way (traffic)   dān xíng xiàn 单行线
DAN-SHEENG CHEEAN

onion   yángcōng   洋葱   YONG-TSONG

open (I)   kāi   开   KI

opera   gējù   歌剧   Guh-Je

operator   jiē xiàn yuán   接线员
    Jee   SHeeN   YooN

orange (color)   júhóng sè   橘红色   Je-HONG Suh

orange (fruit)   chéng zī   橙子   CHONG-Jee

order (I)   diǎncài   点菜   DeeN-TSI

original   zhēng bǎn de   正版的   ZHuNG BaN Duh

owner   yè zhǔ   业主   Ye Joo

oysters   háo (or) mǔ lì   蚝 / 牡蛎
    How   /   Moo-Lee

P

package   bāoguǒ   包裹   Bow-Goo

paid   yǐ fù dè   已付的   ee-Fu Duh

pain   tòng   痛   TONG

painting   huìhuà   绘画   Hoo-Hoo

paper   zhǐ   纸   Juh

parking lot   tíng chē chǎng   停车场
    TONG CHuh CHaNG

partner (business)   shāng wù huǒ bàn
    商务伙伴   SHuNG Woo Hooah BaN

party   jùhuì   聚会   Je-Hoo

passenger   chéng kè   乘客   CHONG-Ke

passport hùzhào 护照 HOO-JOW

pasta tōng xīn fěng 通心粉 TONG SHEEN FONG

pastry gāodiǎn 糕点 GOW-DEEN

pen gāngbǐ 钢笔 GONG-BEE

pencil qiānbǐ 铅笔 CHEEN-BEE

pepper hújiāo fěn 胡椒粉 HOO-JEEOW FON

perfume xiāngshuǐ 香水 SHEEAN-SHOOA

person rén 人 BON

pharmacist yàojì shī 药剂师 YOW-JEE-SHUU

pharmacy yàofáng 药房 YOW-FONG

phone book diàn huà běn 电话本
DEEN HOOA BON

photo zhào piān 照片 ZHOW PEEN

photographer shèyǐng shī 摄影师
SHO-YEENG SHUU

pie (follow with name of filling) pài (or) xiàn bǐng
派 / 馅饼 PY / CHEN-BONG

pillow zhěntou 枕头 ZHON-TO

pink fěn hóng sè 粉红色 FON HONG SO

pizza bǐsà bǐng 比萨饼 BEE-SO BONG

plastic sù liào 塑料 SO-LEEOW

plate pánzi 盘子 PON-ZEE

please qǐng 请 CHONG

pleasure hěn gāo xìng 很高兴 HON GOW SHONG

police jǐngchá 警察 JENG-CHA

police station gōngān jú 公安局
GONG-CHAN JA

pork zhūròu 猪肉 JOO-RO

porter fúwùyuán 服务员 FOO WO YOOAN

post office yóujú 邮局 YO-JA

postcard míng xìn piàn 明信片
MEN SHEN PEEN

potato tǔdòu 土豆 TOO-DO

pregnant huáiyùn 怀孕 HOOI-YAN

prescription yàofāng 药方 YO-FAHNG

price jiàgé 价格 JEEA-GA

problem wèntí 问题 WAN-TA

profession zhíyè 职业 JA-YA

public gōnggòngde 公共的 GONG-GONG

public telephone gōng yòng diàn huà 公用电话
GONG YONG DEEN HOOA

purified chún huà de 纯化的 CHOON-HOOA DUH

purple zǐ sè 紫色 DSEE-SA

purse qiánbāo 钱包 CHEEAN-BOW

Q

quality zhìliàng 质量 JA-LEEANG

question wèntí 问题 WAN-TA

quickly kuài 快 K(oo)(i)

quiet ānjìng 安静 (a)N-J(o)NG

quiet! (be) qǐng ānjìng 请安静 CH(ee)NG (a)N-J(o)NG

R

radio shōuyīnjī 收音机 SH(o)-Y(ee)N-J(ee)

railroad tiělù 铁路 T(ee)(e)-L(oo)

rain xià yǔ (v) SH(ee)(a) Y(oo) 下雨
   yǔ (n) 雨 Y(oo)

raincoat yǔyī 雨衣 Y(oo)-Y(ee)

ramp xié pō 斜坡 SH(ee)(e) P(O)

rare (cooked) nèn 嫩 N(o)N

razor blades dāopiàn 刀片 D(ow)-P(ee)(e)N

ready zhūn bèi hǎo le 准备好了
   J(oo)N B(a) H(ow) L(u)

receipt fāpiào 发票 F(ah)-P(ee)(ow)

recommend (to) tuījiàn 推荐 T(oo)(A)-J(ee)(e)N

red hóng sè 红色 H(o)NG S(u)

repeat! chóngfù 重复 CH(o)NG-F(oo)

reservation yùdìng 预定 Y(oo)-D(e)NG

restaurant fànguǎn 饭馆 F(a)N-G(oo)(a)N

return huán 还 H(oo)(a)N

rice (cooked) mǐfàn 米饭 M(ee)-F(a)N

rich fù yù dè 富裕的 F(oo) Y(oo) D(u)

right (correct)   duì   对   D⓪⓪④

right (direction)   yòu   右   Y⓪

road   mǎlù   马路   Mⓐh-L⓪⓪

room   fángjiān   房间   FⓐNG-JⓔⓔⓔN

round trip   wǎng fǎn   往返   WⓐNG FⓐN

S

safe (hotel)   bǎo xiǎn xiāng   保险箱
B⓪ SHⓔⓔN SHⓔⓔⓐNG

salad   sèlā   色拉   S⓪-Lⓐh

sale   mài   卖   M④

salmon   guī yǔ   鲑鱼   G⓪⓪④ Y⓪⓪

salt   yán   盐   YⓐN

sandwich   sānmíngzhì   三明治   SⓐN-MⓐNG-Jⓔ

Saturday   xīngqī liù   星期六   SHⓔNG-CHⓔ Lⓔⓔ⓪

scissors   jiǎndāo   剪刀   JⓔⓔⓔN-D⓪ⓦ

sculpture   diāosù   雕塑   Dⓔⓔⓞⓦ-S⓪ PⓐN

seafood   hǎixiān   海鲜   H①-SHⓔⓔⓔN

season   jìjié   季节   Jⓔ-Jⓔⓔ⓪

seat   zuò wèi   坐位   DS⓪⓪⓪⓪-W④

secretary   mìshū   秘书   Mⓔ-SH⓪⓪

section   jié   节 (or) zhāng (or)   Jⓔⓔ⓪ JⓐNG

September   jiǔyuè   九月   Jⓔⓔ⓪⓪-Y⓪⓪④

service   fúwù   服务   F⓪-W⓪

several hǎo jǐgè 好几个 HOW JEE-GUH

shampoo xiāngbō 香波 SHEEONG-BO

sheets (bed) chuángdān 床单 CHOONG-DAHN

shirt chènshān 衬衫 CHUN-SHAHN

shoe xié 鞋 SHEE

shoe store xíe diàn 鞋店 SHEE DEEN

shopping center shāng chǎng 商场 SHAHNG-CHAHNG

shower línyù 淋浴 LEN-YOO

shrimp xiā 虾 SHEEAH

sick bìng le 病了 BONG LUH

sign (display) biāo zhì 标志 BEEOW JUH

signature qiānmíng 签名 CHEEEN-MONG

silence! ān jìng! 安静 AHN-JONG

single dānshēn 单身 DAHN-SHUN

sir xiānshēng 先生 SHEEEN-SHONG

sister jiěmèi 姐妹 JEEE-MAY

size dàxiǎo 大小 DAH-SHEEOW

skin pífū 皮肤 PEE-FOO

skirt qúnzi 裙子 CHUN-ZEE

sleeve xiùzi 袖子 SHEEOO-DSEE

slowly màn de 慢地 MON-DUH

small xiǎo 小 SHOW

smile (l)   wēixiào   微笑   WⒶ-SHⒺⒺⓌ

smoke (l)   chōu yān   抽烟   CHⓄ-Yⓐ︎N

soap   féizào   肥皂   FⒶ-ZⓌ

socks   wàzi   袜子   Wⓐ︎-ZⒺⒺ

some   yìxiē   一些   YⒺ-SHⒺⒺⓔ︎

something   yǒu xiē dōng xī   有些东西

     YⓄ   SHⒺⒺⓔ︎   DⓄNG   SHⒺⒺ

sometimes   yǒu shí hòu   有时候   YⓄ-SHⓌ   HⓄ

soon   mǎshàng   马上   Mⓐ︎S-HⓐNG

sorry (l am)   duì bùqǐ   对不起   BⓄⓄⒶ   BⓌ-CHⓌ

soup   tāng   汤   Tⓐ︎NG

south   nán   南   NⓐN

souvenir   jìniànpǐn   纪念品   JⒺⒺ-NⒺⒺⓐ︎N-PⓔN

speciality   zhuān cháng   专长   JⓄⓄⓐ︎N   CHⓐNG

speed   sùdù   速度   SⓌ-DⓌ

spoon   sháozi   勺子   SHⓌ-DSⓊ

sport   yùndòng   运动   YⓌ-DⓄNG

Spring (season)   chūn tiān   春天   CHⓄⓄN   TⒺⒺⓔ︎N

stairs   lóutī   楼梯   LⓄ-TⒺⒺ

stamp   yóupiào   邮票   YⓄ-PⒺⒺⓌ

station   zhàn   站   Jⓐ︎N

steak   niúpái   牛排   NⒺⒺⓊ-PⓍ

steamed   zhēng   蒸   JⓊNG

stop! tíng zhǐ 停止 TING JU

store shāngdiàn 商店 SHANG-DEEN

storm bàofēngyǔ 暴风雨 BOW-FUNG-YU

straight ahead xiàng qián zǒu 向前走
    SHEENG CHEEN DSO

strawberry cǎo méi 草莓 TSOW-MA

street jiē dào 街道 JEEE DOW

string shéngzi 绳子 SHONG-ZEE

subway dìtiě 地铁 DEE-TEEE

sugar táng 糖 TANG

suit (clothes) xīzhuāng 西装 SHEE-JOOANG

suitcase xiāngzi 箱子 SHEEANG-DSUr

Summer xiàjì 夏季 SHEEA-JEE

sun taìyáng 太阳 TO-YANG

suntan lotion fáng shài shuāng 防晒霜
    FANG SHO SHOOANG

Sunday xīngqītiān 星期天 SHEENG-CHEE-TEEEN

sunglasses mò jìng 墨镜 MO-JANG

supermarket chāo shì 超市 CHOW SHU

surprise jīngyà 惊讶 JENG-YA

sweet tián 甜 TEEN

swim (I) yóuyǒng 游泳 YO-YONG

swimming pool yóuyǒng chí 游泳池
    YO-YONG CHE

synagogue   yóutàijiào huìtáng   犹太教会堂
YO-TZ-JEE HOOA-TONG

T

table   zhuō zi   桌子   JOOah DSEE

tampons   wèishēng shuān   卫生栓
WA-SHuNG SHOOahN

tape (sticky)   jiāodài   胶带   JEEah-DZ

tape recorder   lùyīnjī   录音机   LOO-YEEN-JEE

tax   shuì   税   SHOOA

taxi   chūzū qìchē   出租汽车   CHOO-DSOO CHEE-CHuh

tea   chá   茶   CHaa

telegram   diànbào   电报   DEEAN-BOw

telephone   diànhuà   电话   DEEAN-HOOaa

television   diànshì   电视   DEEAN-SHO

temperature   wēndù   温度   WuN-DOO

temple   sìyuàn (or) miào   寺院／庙
SEE-YOOAN ／ MEEw

tennis   wǎng qiú   网球   WahNG-CHEEOO

tennis court   wǎng jiú chǎng   网球场
WahNG CHOOA CHaNG

thank you   xièxie   谢谢   SHEEA-SHEEE

that   nà   那   Naa

the   zhè   这   Juh

theater (movie)   diàn yǐng yuàn   电影院
D(EE)(E)N Y(E)NG Y(OO)(E)N

there   nǎ lǐ   那里   N(A)-L(EE)

they   tāmen   他们   T(ah)-M(uh)N

this   zhè   这   J(uh)

thread   xiàn   线   SH(EE)(E)N

throat   hóulóng   喉咙   H(O)-L(O)NG

Thursday   xīngqī sì   星期四   SH(E)NG-CH(EE) S(EE)

ticket   piào   票   P(EE)(ow)

tie   lǐngdài   领带   L(EE)NG-D(I)

time   shíjiān   时间   SH(E)-J(EE)(E)N

tip (gratuity)   xiǎofèi   消费   SH(EE)(ow)-F(A)

tire   lǔn tāi   轮胎   L(oo)N-T(I)

tired   lèi   累   L(A)

toast (bread)   kǎo miànbāo   烤面包
K(ow) M(EE)(E)N-B(ow)

tobacco   yāncǎo   烟草   Y(ah)N-TS(ow)

today   jīntiān   今天   J(EE)N-T(EE)(E)N

toe   jiǎozhǐ   脚趾   J(EE)(ow)-J(ur)

together   yìqǐ   一起   (E)-CH(EE)

toilet   cèsuǒ   厕所   TS(uh)-S(oo)(o)

toilet paper   weì shēng zhǐ   卫生纸   W(A) SH(uh)NG J(ur)

tomato   fānqié   番茄   F(ah)N-CH(EE)(E)

tomorrow míngtiān 明天 M⊕NG-T㊉㊉N

toothache yáténg 牙疼 Y⊕-T⊕NG

toothbrush yáshuā 牙刷 Y⊕S-SH⊚⊚⊚

toothpaste yá gāo 牙膏 Y⊕-G⊚Ⓦ

toothpick yáqiān 牙签 Y⊕-CH㊉㊉N

tour lǚxíng 旅行 L⊕-SH⊕NG

tourist yóu kè 游客 Y⊚ K⊚

tourist office yóu kè bàn gōng shì 游客办公室
YⓄ K⊚ B⊚N G⊚NG SH⊚

towel máojīn 毛巾 M⊚-J㊉㊉N

train huǒchē 火车 H⊚⊚⊚-CH⊚

travel agency lǚxíng shè 旅行社
L⊕-SH⊕NG SH⊚

traveler's check lǚxíng zhīpiào 旅行支票
L⊕-SH⊕NG J⊕-P㊉⊚

trip lǚxíng 旅行 L⊕-SH⊕NG

trousers kū zi 裤子 K⊚DS

trout zūn yú 鳟鱼 DS⊚⊚N Y⊚

truth zhēnlǐ 真理 J⊕N-L⊚

Tuesday xīngqī èr 星期二 SH㊉㊉NG-CH㊉ ⊚B

turkey huǒjī 火鸡 H⊚⊚⊚-J㊉㊉

U

umbrella yǔsǎn 雨伞 Y⊕-S⊚N

understand (to) lǐ jiě 理解 L㉆ J㉆㉅

underwear nèiyī 内衣 N④-㉆

United States Měi Guó 美国 M④-G⑩⑩

university dàxué 大学 D⑭-SH⑩⑥

up shàng 上 SH⑭NG

urgent jǐn jí 紧急 J㉆N J㉆

V

vacant kòng xiánde 空闲的 K⓪NG SH㉆⑭N-D⑭

vacation dù jià 度假 D⑩ J㉆⑭

valuable guì zhòng de 贵重的 G⑩④ J⓪NG D⑭

value jiàzhí 价值 J㉆⑭-J㉆

vanilla xiāng cǎo 香草 SH㉆⑭NG TS⑭

veal xiǎo niú ròu 小牛肉 SH㉆⑭ N㉆⑩ B⓪

vegetables shūcài 蔬菜 SH⑩-TS②

view jǐngsè 景色 J㉆NG-S⑭

vinegar cù 醋 TS⑩

voyage hángxíng 航行 H⓪NG-SH⑭NG

W

wait! děng 等 D⑭NG

waiter / waitress fúwùyuán 服务员
F⑩-W⑭-Y⑩⑭N

want (I) yào 要 Y⑭

wash (I) xǐ 洗 SH㉆

watch out! xiǎoxīn 小心 SHEE-SHEEN

water shuǐ 水 SHOOA

watermelon xī guā 西瓜 SHEE GOOah

we wǒmen 我们 Wah-MuhN

weather tiān qì 天气 TEEEN-GEE

Wednesday xīng qī sān 星期三
    SHENG CHEE SahN

week xīng qī 星期 SHENG-CHEE

weekend zhōumò 周末 JO-MO

welcome huānyíng 欢迎 HOOahN-YENG

well done (cooked) lǎo 老 LaoW

west xī 西 SHEE

wheelchair lún yǐ 轮椅 LuN-EE

when? shènme shíhòu 什么时候
    SHuhN-Muh SHOO-HO

where nǎ li 哪里 Nah LEE

which? nǎ gè 哪个 Nah-GUh

white bái 白 BO

who? shuí 谁 SHOOA

why? wèishénme 为什么 WA-SHuhN-MuH

wife qī zi 妻子 CHEE-Zuh

wind fēng 风 FuhNG

window chuāng 窗 CHOOahNG

wine list jiǔ dān 酒单 JEE⑩ DEEⓔN

wine pú táo jiǔ 葡萄酒 P⑩-T⑭ JEE⑩

Winter dōngjì 冬季 D⑩NG-Jⓔ

with gēn / hé / yǔ (formal) 跟 / 和 / 与
GⓤN / H⑩ / Yⓔ

woman nǔ rén 女人 Nⓔ BⓔN

wonderful tài hǎo le 太好了 TⓄ H⑩ Lⓤ

world shìjiè 世界 SHⓄ-JEEⓔ

wrong cuò-le 错了 TS⑩Ⓐ Lⓤ

XYZ

year nián 年 NEEⓈN

yellow huáng sè 黄色 H⑩Ⓐ NG Sⓔ

yes shì 是 SHⓄ Dⓤ

yesterday zuótiān 昨天 DS⑩Ⓐ-TEEⓔN

you nǐ 你 Nⓔ

zipper lāliàn 拉链 LⓐⒽLEEⓔN

zoo dòngwùyuán 动物园 D⑩NG-W⑩-Y⑩ⓈN

EASILY PRONOUNCED LANGUAGE SYSTEMS

Author Clyde Peters graduated from Radford High School and the University of Hawaii and has traveled the world as a travel writer. His innovative Say It Right phrase books have revolutionized the way languages are taught and learned. Mr. Peters invented the Vowel Symbol System for easy and correct pronunciation of virtually any language. He currently continues traveling the world working on new languages and divides his spare time between Las Vegas, Nevada, and Hawaii.

Betty Chapman is a successful business woman who along with Mr. Peters founded Easily Pronounced Language Systems to promote education, travel, and custom tailored language solutions. "Moving beyond expectation to acquisition and accomplishment is possible with EPLS."

Priscilla Leal Bailey is the senior series editor for all Say It Right products and has proved indispensable in editing and implementing the EPLS Vowel Symbol System. We are forever grateful for her belief and support.

SAY IT RIGHT SERIES
Infinite Destinations
One Pronunciation System!

Audio Editions

Say It Right App on iTunes

179

THANKS!

The nicest thing you can say to anyone in any language is "Thank you." Try some of these languages using the incredible EPLS Vowel Symbol System.

Arabic

SH00-KR@N

Chinese

SH€€€ SH€€€

French

M®B-S€€

German

D@N-K@

Hawaiian

M@-H@-L0

Italian

GR@T-S€€-®

Japanese

D0-M0

Portuguese

0-BR€€-G@-D0

Russian

SP@-S€€-B@

Spanish

GR@-S€€-@S

Swahili

@-S@N-T@

Tagalog

S@-L@-M@T

INDEX

QUICK REFERENCE PAGE

Hello

Nǐ hǎo!   你好

N㉺ H㉾

How are you?

Nǐ hǎo ma?   你好吗？

N㉺ H㉾ M㉮

Yes

Shì   是

SH㉾

No

Bú shì   不是

B㉺ SH㉾

Please

Qǐng   请

CH㉾NG

Thank you

Xiè xie nǐ   谢谢你

SH㉺㉾ SH㉺㉾ N㉺

I'm sorry.

Duìbù qǐ.   对不起

D㉺㉮-B㉺ CH㉺

I don't understand.

Wǒ bù dǒng.   我不懂

W㉮ B㉺ D㉿NG

Help!

Jiù mìng!   救命！

J㉺㉺NG M㉾NG
